DAD

DAD

AUBREY MALONE

First published December 2025

ISBN 978-1-913144-73-9

Cover:

PENNILESS PRESS PUBLICATIONS
Website:www.pennilesspress.co.uk/books

Acknowledgements

Thank you to various members of my family for jogging my memory regarding the various anecdotes in this book. Any misrememberings are my own.

A special thanks to Basil for all the photographs from his vast archives, and to Ken Clay as ever for his herculean labours in collating the various elements of the book.

The past is another country. They do things differently there.

L.P. Hartley

Introduction

Even when I was very young I knew my father was different from everyone else's one. He dressed different and talked different and he had a way of carrying himself that seemed to say he represented something unusual, something that was going to make people stop what they were doing to look at him.

The problem with standing out in a town the size of ours was that you made yourself into a target. He liked the attention but not all that it entailed. Bright lights attract moths. They also attract people who want to make them darker, or break them. When you climb a hill you can be shot down.

Some people are better at dealing with these kinds of situations than others. The ones who put themselves about like my father did usually have thick skins. He didn't. It hurt him when people criticised him or asked questions about where he came from or where his father came from or how he got to be where he was.

He acted indifferent to these kinds of comments when he was in public but at home it was different. My mother knew how much they affected him. She tried to get him to let them run off him but she didn't always succeed. He took the hurt into himself.

It built up over the years. Eventually he reached a situation where he felt he had to leave the town. He was 65 at that time. I was only a teenager. We were both equally torn. He was leaving because he felt he had to rather than wanted to and I was the same.

Every ending is a new beginning just as every sunset brings a new dawn. If we're lucky we can reconstruct the things we left behind in a different way. We made a life for ourselves in Dublin. The house we moved into became a substitute for the Ballina one. Many of the family were in it. That helped, but nothing can substitute for the connections we make in our childhood.

My father pined for the past. He talked so much about his own father that I became impatient with him. Little did I realise that I'd be doing almost exactly the same thing years later in a book.

Maybe all sons turn into their fathers in time. Or maybe I just caught the dust off the spell he wove, the spell of his recitations and dissertations, becoming a Boswell to his Johnson, tracing his path from country to city as he folded the tent on his career and embarked on the third phase of his life.

He put the world on watch like a defendant in the dock from the eyrie of his bedroom in Glasnevin, looking out the double doors into the glasshouse as he reminisced. We sat at his feet taking it all in, wondering if the past was really as magical as he made it out to be or if he romanticised it too much, creating sermons out of the stones as he told us how shabby it was in comparison to the present.

Memories, as the song says, sweeten through the ages just like wine. This is the story of how he tried to pit the present against that past as he conjured up a time he was never going to be able to recapture during the last decade of his life.

Origins

I never knew much about my father's early years. Like most sons, I didn't express much interest when he talked about them. I was too busy with my life.

I don't know where he went to Primary School or anything else about those years. All I know is that he boarded in secondary schools in Blackrock and Castleknock. His father, Patrick Joseph Malone, was a Justice of the Peace. When he was writing his name he used to write 'PJ Malone, JP.' It was almost the same back to front.

He was born in 1850, not long after the Famine. As well as being a judge he was a Poor Law Guardian, a church leader and a harbourmaster.

My father was in awe of him. It was an awe, I think, that was sometimes tinged with fear.

He owned a lot of properties around Ballina. I asked my father how he came to have so many of them.

'He knew when to buy and when to sell,' he said, 'It's as simple as that. Keeping your eye on the market for what's going to increase in price and what isn't. Once you get your foot on the ladder you're away with it.'

My grandfather made his fortune in what my father called 'the rag trade.' It enabled him to branch out in all those different directions and secure his future.

He owned one of the first cars in the county. My father told me he picked up a hitch-hiker one day. After the man sat into the car he asked him where he was going.

'I'm not going anywhere,' he replied, 'I just wanted to know what it felt like to be in a car.'

It was said he rode into town on an ass and cart as a young man. My father claimed that was a story concocted to pull him down. He said people in small towns were always trying to pull you down.

He preferred talking about the successes his father had, how fair he was with people.

'He gave everyone twenty shillings to the pound,' he said.

I didn't care if he rode into town in an ass and cart or not. If he did, it made him better in my eyes than someone who was born with a silver spoon in their mouth.

He gave us articles about him that had been printed in the 'Western People,' our local paper.

One of them showed him at the unveiling of the Humbert Monument.

Maud Gonne MacBride performed the ceremony. I used to think it was Countess Markiewicz. It took place in 1898, the centenary of the 1798 rebellion of the United Irishmen against the British.

A French general, Jean Joseph Humbert, had led a column of French and Irish soldiers through Belleek.

They had a famous victory against the British there, one that's still talked about in the town and proudly remembered by Irish people everywhere.

My grandfather married three times. All three of his wives had Mary in their names. His first two predeceased him, the third outliving him. That wasn't surprising as he was nearly twenty years older than her.

One day I asked my father who'd be his real wife in heaven.

'I can't answer that,' he said.

When I asked him how he felt about his father marrying three times, all he said was, 'That's a triumph of hope over experience.'

He didn't talk much about the first two families. I heard once that the son of his first wife got a girl 'into trouble,' in other words pregnant. Tongues wagged around the town

My grandparents

about him so he had to be removed from it. Problems of that kind were brushed under the carpet at the time. He was packed off to America with the proverbial shilling. The girl disappeared too. She would have been seen as 'damaged goods.'

My grandfather's first two wives were called Bridget Mary Cullen and Mary McCarthy. The third one, Mary Ellen Dillon, wanted the Dillon to be appended to Malone to distinguish her family from his others. As a result, my father and his siblings grew up as Dillon-Malones.

His Christian name was Hugh. He had a brother, Louis, and two sisters, Mary and Nellie. Uncle Louis became a doctor. He moved to Birmingham after getting married. I don't ever remember seeing him.

Mary married a wealthy man called Eddie Murphy. He owned a flour mill in Bunree, an area of Ballina down by the swimming pool. She was an angelic-looking woman with an austere way about her. I often saw her in the cathedral saying the stations. She reminded me of a silent movie queen.

When we were young we used to go down to Bunree to see her. She had five children with Uncle Eddie: Paddy, Edward, Feena, Brian and Jimmy. They had a tennis in their grounds and a lot of land with vegetables. We used to pick strawberries there and sell them to a shop in King Street.

Aunt Nellie didn't marry. She lived near us on the Killala Road. Her house was called Feamore. She was up and down to us all the time. She wore a fur coat and enough perfume to knock you out as she swaggered her way up Arthur Street to see us.

We used to go down to her as well. Whenever we couldn't find something in Norfolk we used to say, 'Maybe

My grandfather, P.J. Malone

it's in Aunt Nellie's room behind the wallpaper.' I never knew why.

My father told me lots of stories about her. He said she was a tearaway when she was young. She was sent to boarding school to try and knock that out of her.

'She used to cry her eyes out to avoid going back after the holidays,' he said. As soon as the train pulled out of the station she'd already be laughing with her friends.

When she got to the school she'd be back to her wild ways. After leaving one convent to go to another one once, the Reverend Mother greeted her with the words, 'Your reputation has preceded you.'

My father was too similar to her in personality to get on with her. They flashed off one another. Both of them had tempers. Aunt Nellie had red hair to go with it. He had a tinge of it too, leading to him being called 'Red Hugh' by some people.

'We love one another from a distance,' he used to say, 'We're cut from a different cloth.' They couldn't be in a room for more than five minutes together before they'd start arguing about something. My mother usually acted as 'referee.'

We lived in a big house on Arthur Street. There were nine of us altogether, leading to our father referring to us as his 'novena.' I was the youngest. Our previous house was around the corner on Convent Hill. Before that my parents lived in Greystones in County Wicklow. That was where they got married. My father was a student in Trinity College at the time.

Being a Catholic, he had to get a dispensation to go there. 'Trinity' was primarily a Protestant college at that time. He had his own room, Number 9. Most of his friends were 'C of E' as he put it. This was in the days when most of us thought Protestants were like some weird species from outer space. I didn't know any when I was growing up. He never had a problem with them. They even used to call him for Mass sometimes. Some of them were from the North. 'It's a different culture up there,' he said to me. 'A person from Dublin will ask you how you're doing. A person from Belfast will say, 'How is business?'

He wasn't that interested in studying. Because his father was wealthy, there was no pressure on him to graduate. He spent a lot of his time partying. 'We'd swing on the gates of the college,' he told me, 'watching the girls going up and down Grafton Street. The future was a long way away.'

He was studying law but spent more time drinking than studying. It was like Oscar Wilde's saying, 'Work is the curse of the drinking classes.'

'I started out for one bar,' he said, 'and ended up at another one.' Another gag was, 'I took more pledges than drink.' One of his friends from the class said, 'I go to bed every night an alcoholic and wake up a pioneer.'

He had a friend called Mido Cooligan. Mido joined him in his 'Scott Fitzgerald' lifestyle. At the end of each academic year the pair of them would go up to the results board.

As my father scanned it, Mido would say to him, 'I don't know why you're bothering. You know you're down to hell.' He used to chortle at this.

Any time he ran short of money his mother baled him out. 'Mother,' as he referred to her, had a soft spot for him. Her attitude was that it was there so why not use it.

His father was more stern. I heard once that he said to him once when he was home in Ballina on a break, 'If the stories I hear about you in Dublin are true, I'd prefer if someone else walked through that door than yourself.'

My father was still a student when he got married. He was 31 years of age. My mother was 24. Her name was Patricia Conry. She came from a place called Raheen in County Roscommon.

'Pat was from a county family,' he boasted, 'She rode to the hounds.' He said he fell in love with her and then took a peep into her background. 'That made me love her even more,' he said.

He was always making these kinds of jokes against himself. Another one was this quip to my mother, 'I love you more than the sun, the moon and the stars - and I'll be up to see you tomorrow if it isn't raining.'

Her father was a gentleman farmer but the family was coming down in the world when he met her. One day, she told me, her father wrote a cheque that bounced.

He couldn't believe it. It was the first sign that their world was changing. Raheen would later become a ruin.

My father's first date with her was on a boat. It was a windy day and the sea was choppy. He clutched the edges of the boat nervously as he wasn't used to being on the water. My mother was amused by him. She hadn't a nerve in her body then. 'She'd stay cool in a hurricane,' he said.

He had a better chance to use his silver tongue on her when he got her back on 'terra firma,' chasing her across the hills and dales of Roscommon until she agreed to marry him. Marriage was the last thing on her mind at the time.

'I wore her down eventually,' he said. He became a different person when he had an audience in front of him.

He wasn't a great prospect then, having spent so much time in Trinity without anything to show for it, but he charmed her with his personality. He also charmed her mother. Both of them loved listening to his stories.

My mother was shy by nature. He relaxed her.

He was shy too but he hid it. When he went to functions with her he was able to talk to everyone under the table. It put her at her ease. Before she knew it he'd have introduced her to half the people there.

He wasn't tall in stature but he had presence. The U2 singer Bono once said the stage was his platform sole, that it

My grandmother, Ellen Dillon

gave him an invisible six inches in his psychological height. My father probably felt the same.

Their backgrounds were so different. Her country one meant she wasn't sophisticated but she had something more important – class. Not just social class, something I never cared about, but in her character. She got some words wrong when she was writing letters and that amused him. He enjoyed teaching her things.

Their personalities were also light years apart. He was the colourful one telling stories at parties and she was the one who worried about him saying too much. He talked and she listened. He blew up and she kept calm. He had the nerves and she had the tranquillity.

They got married in 1935. The fact that he was seven years older than her meant she'd had less boyfriends than he'd had girlfriends. That didn't seem to matter to her. Once she fell for him, that was it. It was the same for him but I don't think he'd have been ready for marriage at her age of 24. He had too much living to do.

I never saw a wedding photo. I doubt there was one taken. He suggested to me once that they eloped. Perhaps her father disapproved of him, not being as easily won over by him as her mother.

I imagine them standing in a church at dawn, each of them dressed in ordinary clothes, the ceremony being performed with little or no notice being given to the priest. I can't see any guests being there and I don't know who the best man would have been. They were just two people starting out on their life together, not thinking of careers or children or anything else.

I don't remember either of them ever telling me they had a honeymoon. There might have been a day trip somewhere or a meal out but that would have been it.

They spent the first months of married life in a house in Greystones called Fuschia Cottage. My oldest brother Keith was born there. He liked to boast about being the only member of the family who was born in Dublin. I don't know why. I wouldn't have boasted about that if it was me.

Keith was only two when World War I broke out. It didn't come to Ireland but my father talked a lot about it. How could you not?

England asked us for its support against 'The Hun.' Some of us, as the saying went, 'took the shilling' and joined their army. Others couldn't forget the 800 years of suppression under The Old Enemy. They thought: Why should we care if Hitler attacked the nation that brutalised us?

But of course if he got into England, we were next. The decision to fight or not to fight with them became like a mini Civil War among us. We were good at those. As Brendan Behan once said, the first item on the agenda of any Irish meeting is The Split.

There's a photograph of my mother and father crossing O'Connell Bridge later on in this book. It was probably taken around the time of the war. I imagine the photographer was a man who used to stand all day on the bridge snapping people.

He would have been that time's equivalent of the paparazzi except for the fact that he photographed 'ordinary' people instead of celebrities. He gave you his card and if you wanted the photograph you went into his office a few days later and saw it in a sea of transparencies laid out on his counter.

I was often annoyed by him whenever he stopped me but in later years I found myself becoming grateful to him. He gave us keepsakes of our lives, of the lives of people who came before us. When I look at my father in that photograph I see him at a changing point in his life, becoming more serious. His party self was going into abeyance and real life, whatever that was, starting to intrude.

He started to knuckle down to his studies after he got married. It was time for him. As he put it, 'I wasn't getting any smarter and the exams weren't getting any easier.' He'd been over a decade at Trinity at this stage. Maybe he was even older than some of his lecturers.

What would my grandfather have thought of him taking ten years to graduate? What would Uncle Louis have thought? He was well on the road in his medical career at this stage.

I wish I asked my father these questions as I was growing up. I knew people in genealogical societies who went back several generations to find out how their ancestors lived. I could hardly go back even one. All I knew was that he was about to embark on a new life with his new wife.

No longer would he be a gadabout. No longer would parties go on all night. The days of going up to the results board with Mido Cooligan and hearing him say he was 'down to hell' were at an end.

Solicitor

My father went back to Ballina to set up a legal practice after graduating from Trinity. He bought the house on Convent Hill then, living there with my mother and Keith as he saved up for a bigger one. He said to her one day, 'I'm going to be a State solicitor.'

He had an office in Bridge Street. It was near the Moy river. He used to walk down to it every day in his Trinity gear - a pinstriped suit with a handkerchief in the lapel of the jacket and a waistcoat with a fob pocket for his watch.

He also wore a white scarf. I saw these in films sometimes. I wondered if that was where he got the idea. Edward G. Robinson, or Edward Robinson as he called him, used to wear them in gangster films.

To many people he came across as a dandy. He liked quoting the lines of W.F. Hargreaves, 'I'm Berlington Bertie, I rise at ten thirty and saunter along like a toff. I walk down the Strand with my gloves in my hand and then down again with them off.'

He wore garters on the elbows of his shirts. The collars and cuffs were dislodgeable. The whole package gave him an image. It was as if he still thought he was in Trinity. With the outfit came confidence. He reverted to the young man he'd been in his twenties. In bars and hotels he performed for anyone who was there, telling the same stories over and over.

The courthouse acted as another 'venue' for him to perform. He went up to it with a spring in his step every time he had a case. It didn't matter if it was big or small. Sometimes he was just awarded the proverbial penny. Other times he toughed things until, as he put it, 'The longest purse won.' He gave each case everything he had. To him the

My grandfather

courthouse was like the Old Bailey. He made something out of nothing in it time and again with his theatricality.

He had that image outside it as well. His mode of dress accentuated it. To quote Shakespeare, the apparel made the man.

He carried an umbrella even when it wasn't raining. The Bertie-esque gloves, like the waistcoat, were worn even when the weather was hot. Such indulgences were almost masochistic. He must have really sweated when the sun was shining.

One year there was a poem written about him in the 'Western' called 'The Brolly Brigade.' 'Hugh Dillon-Malone,' it began, 'so gracefully growing old.' It was written by a person who called themselves Sean Bocht. We never found out who it was. My father didn't do anything about it.

'Who do you think wrote it? I asked him one day. 'I don't know and I don't care,' he said, 'It was probably somebody who thinks I'm trying to be Lord Knock'em Stiff. Put a beggar on horseback.'

I felt he was more upset about it than he pretended. 'That's what happens in small towns,' he said, 'It's like when they said my father came here on a donkey and cart. A paper never refuses ink.'

He told me a story about a man who was abused in a bar one night. The next day the person who insulted him said, 'Sorry for insulting you.' The man replied, 'You didn't insult me. You offered me an insult but I didn't accept it.'

He told another story about a man from Galway whose name was Joyce. He was called 'Butcher' by an enemy of his in a pub one night. Apparently he was ruthless in his dealings with people. The nickname alluded to that. Joyce went to a solicitor and sued him for slander.

Raheen

He won the case but it was, he said, a 'pyrrhic' victory. 'Before he took the case,' he said, 'it was only the people in the bar who heard the slur. Afterwards everyone in the county knew about it.' He said it was always better to ignore these things. When the eagles were silent, the parrots jabbered.

As well as having all the Trinty gear, he also wore a monocle. Apparently he'd been diagnosed as having a weak eye once.

'I couldn't wait to get to an optician to buy one,' he confessed. It gave him the look of a person of high rank. He kept it on a string that he wore round his neck. When he widened his eye it popped out.

Tina Walsh's brother Marty told me that he saw him using it to good effect outside a hotel one night. Some teddy boys, or 'teddy bears' as he called them, were smirking at him. One of them called him 'The Penguin.' This was a character out of 'Batman,' a series that was showing on television at the time. My father stopped in his tracks. He put in his monocle and withered them with a look. It worked, causing them to scamper off.

Afterwards he went into the hotel to tell people what happened. He bought drinks on the house. This could have been construed as showing off. I saw it more as a shy man relieved that he'd dodged a bullet.

Marty's wife Mary worked in the hotel. She told me he gave her a ten shilling note once for a tip. 'That was like a week's wages to me then,' she said.

My mother worried about him being theatrical in public places. She saw him spending money that could have been used for groceries to feed the nine of us. Because he was pound foolish she had to be penny wise.

I felt our double-barrelled name didn't suit us. We didn't have the money to back it up. Today every Tom, Dick or Harry has one but in those days it was rare.

My father in uncharacteristically ordinary clothes

He asked me never to tell people where it came from. 'To explain is to apologise,' he said, 'It's none of anyone's business.'

His image was huge for him. If anyone challenged it they became a threat to him. The only way to counteract them, he claimed, was to rise above them.

'There are two kinds of people in the world,' he said, 'One of them walks down Bond Street as if he owns it. The other one walks down Bond Street as if he doesn't care who owns it.' I didn't know which he was.

After we were in the Arthur Street house for a few years he had the house painted in my mother's riding colours of yellow and black. He called it Norfolk. 'The Duke of Norfolk is the only person who doesn't have to stand when the Queen enters a room,' he said. Such details impressed him.

He had many pro-British attitudes. They were probably a result of the fact that his father did so well under what he called the 'ancien regime.' I grew up believing the 1916 Rising was a triviality. One night, someone told me, an IRA man pulled a gun on him in a pub when he started to sing 'God Save the Queen.'

There were four bedrooms in Norfolk. It also had a little boxroom upstairs.

You could get onto the roof from one of the bedrooms. I used to love sitting on it. One day Feena Murphy's son Keelin came to the house. He said, 'Where's Aubrey?' Nobody knew where to find me until they eventually looked on the roof. It led to a wall where you could jump onto a sycamore tree that was in our back yard. We used to lower ropes from it sometimes from the crook and have boxes of food sent up to us.

Gildy Ahern's orchard was on the other side of the wall. We robbed apples from it. One day he chased after us with a pop gun. His house was like a ruin. I was terrified every time I walked past it.

Gildy terrified me too. People made up all sorts of stories about him, saying he killed his wife and children and buried them under the floorboards. It was only in later years I learned he was a gentle soul.

Downstairs in Norfolk was the sitting room. It was the so-called 'good' room where posh visitors waited but we used it for everything. There were too many of us not to. There was also the dining room and a long corridor into the kitchen. This was where my mother relaxed when her morning's work was done, sipping 'bottomless' cups of tea she heated on the range.

There was a piano in the sitting room. My mother used to go in there and play it whenever she was stressed. We also had a wireless in there. It was huge, almost the size of a small fridge. When you turned it on it lit up like the fairy lights of a Christmas tree.

We listened mainly to Radio Luxembourg, the 'station of the stars,' twirling the knob to frequency 208, the magic number. Sunday night was my favourite time for listening to it. That was when the Top Twenty was on. It was good other days as well. I liked Elvis Presley songs the most, especially 'Are You Lonesome Tonight.' That song sent shivers down my spine. We played it on our record player as well. I loved listening to the scratching of the needle when you put it on before he started singing. The radio was like television for a later generation. On Jacinta's birthday in 1964 we 'watched' Cassius Clay beat Sonny Liston on it in the middle of the night.

There was a room above the kitchen that we called the loft. It was a kind of attic. I never knew anyone else that had an attic above their kitchen. It was a bit ramshackle but we loved it. We played lot of games up there. It wasn't that high off the ground.

The kitchen led onto our back yard. That was where we played most of our games – soccer and Queenie and handball and others. There was no grass in it, just clay, but we still played golf on it sometimes, making holes in the clay and using it as a putting area. The ball used to bobble on its way to the hole even if you played it right.

I don't know where the putter came from. Maybe my father played golf as a young man. We found the balls ourselves. I used to go up to the golf links sometimes to see if I could find stray ones in the long grass at the edge of it. If the players sent one in there they usually got fed up looking for it after a while.

There was a garage to the right of our house. We didn't have a car so we used it to store turf. Above it was our next door neighbour's top window. They left it open a lot. The ball used to disappear into it sometimes when we were playing handball. Once or twice we broke the window. Maybe that's why they left it open. If they were in a good mood they threw it back to us, or 'pegged' it back as my mother put it.

At the front of the house above the garage there was an arch separating their property from ours. It was about half an inch wide. They used to paint it in their colours and then we'd go over it in ours. This went on for years. We used up many buckets of paint between us going over one another's handiwork. It was stupid for such a small area. I don't know why it got us worked up so much. Maybe it was because it was at the front of the house. My father used to say, 'An inch on a man's nose is a big thing.'

Some of his cases in court involved people haggling over tiny areas. People guarded their precious turf. A man in Kerry had been shot over ownership of a field in a famous John B. Keane play. I wondered if he might ever be called

With two friends

upon to go to court over the arch. Stranger things had happened.

Across the road from us was the old school. There was also a fire station and a place where they made headstones. Further down was Cottrell's house, then Leonard's, then Syron's where we used to get chips. Fahy's shop was at the corner of Garden Street.

The Cottrells left Ballina in 1965. It was the first big change on the street. They were a large family like ours. I was mainly friends with Edward but I knew them all. We were in one another's houses all the time. They mainly came to ours because of the large playing area we had at the back. I wondered who would be the next family to leave. Little did I know then that it would be us.

Up the road at the other end was the Estoria cinema. The font was beside it. Horses used to stop there for drinks of water in the old days. It had a crazy pavement around it. The stones were all in strange triangular shapes.

Jimmy Geraghty's grocery shop was across the road from Fahy's. It was where we did most of our shopping. We never brought money with us, just a little red book. Mr Geraghty would write down the price of the things we bought. This was often in indecipherable writing. At the end of a month my father would pay him.

We usually got a 'cut' because of our good business. He'd think up a figure. Nobody seemed to be too bothered whether it related to the purchases or not.

Children

Over the next number of years the children started to arrive. My mother was pregnant thirteen times between 1937 and 1953. She once said the only holidays she got were in hospital giving birth.

After Keith there was Clive. Then June came along, the first girl in the family. 'Mare and filly doing well,' my father said when he went to the maternity ward of the hospital.

June was born on the last day of May. 'The last of May saw the first of June,' he said. That was the reason for her name.

Keith was named after G.K. Chesterton, one of his favourite writers. He also liked Graham Greene and Evelyn Waugh, two converts to Catholicism. Was that part of the reason? Maybe.

He was fascinated by the fact that Greene had played Russian Roulette. The other writers he read were people like Hilaire Belloc, Rudyard Kipling, Arthur Conan Doyle. He liked thrillers by Edgar Wallace and Sexton Blake. He read the memoirs of brigadier generals, the war journals of people like Rommel, the so-called 'Desert Fox.'

There were lots of his books around the house when I was growing up, mainly orange-covered paperbacks that he kept in a cabinet in the front room.

They were so small you could fit them in your pocket. I rarely opened them but I was fascinated by the titles, titles like, 'The Man Who Watched the Trains Go By' and 'When the Kissing Had to Stop.' Many of them had a musty smell, the smell of yesterday, of all the yesterdays, of a life when there was nothing to do all day but read.

Ruth was born the year after June. Then there were two boys, Hugo and Basil, and then two more girls, Audrey and

Jacinta. I arrived three years after Jacinta. From that point of view I was probably a surprise.

In the preceding years there was also a miscarriage, a stillborn birth and a set of twins, Raymond and Mary, who only lived a week. As regards those of us who survived there were four sets of what were called 'Irish' twins, i.e. children separated by a year or so. Sometimes the older one was kept back in school so the younger one could be in the same class as them.

Ernest Hemingway once said, 'When you become a father there's one absolute rule. You must not look at your child for the first two years.' I don't remember my father much in my early years. He certainly wasn't the type of man to change a nappy. Not many fathers did in those days.

Nine was large for a family, even a Catholic one. Family planning wasn't thought of then. If you had more children than you bargained for you had to find a way to feed and clothe them. It was as simple as that.

I imagine my father surprised himself by how well he took to a life of routine after the excitement of Trinity. Maybe we all find our water level eventually. The study in Trinity was a chore until he met my mother. Then it became a labour of love.

After I was born my mother employed a girl to, as she put it, get me out from under her feet. Her name was Tina Walsh. Tina was only meant to be with us for a fortnight but she ended up staying sixteen years. She became like a second mother to me.

I was five before I started school. June coached me at home so I went straight from Junior Infants, which was then called Small Babies, into what was called Low First. That early achievement confirmed my father in his view that, like all his other children, I was blessed by genius.

I was quiet as a child. Maybe that was because he was so talkative. Everyone else in the family talked a lot as well.

You had to fight to get a word in edgewise. That's what happens in large families. Bob Hope once said that he learned to dance as a child as a result of waiting to get into the toilet. That was another problem. We grew up in an age before en-suites.

As well as the nine of us there was a cat called Tabby. She used to claw at the couch anytime it was going to rain. She was better than any weather forecaster at predicting it. She disappeared for long periods to places and then came back unexpectedly.

We also had a dog, Deezer. He was a cross between a setter and a pointer. We rescued him from a house in Lord Edward Street one day where he was being starved by his owner. He had him tethered to a chain link fence. The rope around his neck almost strangled him.

We told him we were going to report him to the RSPCA unless he sold him to us. He was skin and bone. When we got him to back to Norfolk he jumped up on the table and ate everyone's dinner. I brought him for walks down Arthur Street and other places like Convent Hill. There weren't many cars around in those days so it was safe.

On Fair Days you'd hear donkeys braying outside our front windows. You'd see farmers spitting on their hands as they made deals. They'd pretend to walk away from them if the price they were asking for their cattle was deemed to be too low.

The sounds would thin out as the day went on. By night all that would be left on the street were cowpats. It would be as silent as a grave when I went to sleep in the boxroom of our house. The music from the Town Hall for once, wouldn't be lulling me to sleep. The dances that were usually held there would be cancelled because of the Fair Day.

The next morning it would all begin again, the cacophony coming in through the curtains, people calling out to one another in the street, people going to work, cars whizzing up and down, horns honking at pedestrians as I got myself ready for my Golgotha-like cycle to Muredach's over the potholed roads.

My parents with Keith as a baby

Ballina

Ballina reminded me of the small American towns we saw in the films in the Estoria. Everything was tabulated. We went up to Arthur Wills for our milk. He gave us a bit extra for the cat, pouring it into the tin bucket with his ladle. We went to Geraghty's for our groceries, to Brennan's for our comics, to Clarke's for our newspapers. We got the punctures in our bikes fixed by Tommy Ward at the end of the street. If we wasn't there we went up to Lynn's on Lord Edward Street.

We got chips in Syron's or the Royal Café and records in Byron's. We got everything from a needle to an anchor in Woolworth's. If they didn't have what we wanted, we went down to Wellworth's near my father's office. It was like Woolworth's except it didn't have as many things.

We got our clothes in Gavin's or Hanley's and our shoes in Queenan's. There was a shop near the Market Square that sold jewellery. The man who owned it had a red face and a ball head shaped like a rugby ball, saying to customers, 'What can I do for you?' I never saw him anywhere else but behind the counter. It was as if that was his only existence. I felt that if I left the town and came back in twenty years he'd still be standing behind the counter looking the same as ever and saying to customers, 'What can I do for you?'

Curly's shop sold clothes. It was beside Tom MacDonnells' electrical shop on Garden Street. Courell's was further down. If you wanted curtains, Mr Courell would roll them out for you on his counter to let you see the patterns. Across the road from him was the dry cleaners run by the Loftuses. We got our toys from Benny Walkin's shop, the International Stores. One of his brothers had a fishing tackle place near it.

I couldn't imagine any of us wanting anything that was on sale in any of these places. If they didn't have it they'd get it for us from Crossmolina or Foxford or Westport or Belmullet.

Norfolk like an open house. People visited at all hours of the day and night, people like the O'Horas, the Cahills, the Cottrells and the Courells, and Sean MacDonnell, Tom's son from Garden Street. My father called him 'Mac.' He did odd jobs for us.

People sometimes knocked on the door on the way home from the Estoria. My father knew the manager, Paddy Mulligan. He often got free passes from him for us. In return he did some work for him. It was what he called a 'contra' arrangement. It was great getting in for nothing. People sometimes tried to 'duke in,' as they put it, by the back door but they were usually caught.

I liked looking at the posters outside the Estoria. Sometimes they were more exciting than the films they advertised. They'd show scenes from the film in sizzling colour. Heroes would be dashing blades. Heroines would have figures like from comics with exaggerated bosoms and thighs. You'd see sabres and gatling guns and cliff edges and waterfalls and people hanging off the edges of aeroplanes.

My father was bringing us to the Estoria almost from the cradle. Other families had days set aside to go to 'the pictures.' With us, the days we didn't go were almost the exceptions.

If we weren't seeing films we were talking about them or thinking about them. When other families discussed the state of the nation, we discussed people like Robert Mitchum and Randolph Scott and Grace Kelly. I hardly even knew who was in power in the government. When someone mentioned Fianna Fáil to me once I thought they meant my godmother had a tumble – 'Feena Fall.'

I went to Westerns and war films and Arabian Nights ones. When I came out of the Estoria it blotted out all the bad things that had happened that day or that week or that month. I was with Gregory Peck in Navarone, with Alec Guinness on the bridge on the River Kwai, with John Wayne in Monument Valley, with Douglas Fairbanks in the French Foreign Legion.

The teachers in Muredach's didn't like us going to films at night. They thought it would make us sleepy at our lessons the next day, or that the curvaceous women in them would give us 'bad thoughts.'

I dreaded the Mission priests who came to the Cathedral each year. They told us we'd be damned to hell if we had any such thoughts. We were never warned against murdering people or robbing banks. Only the sins of the flesh mattered. With anything else, it seemed, you'd be safe from Lucifer's cloven hoof.

My father had an unusual attitude to films. If he missed even a minute at the beginning it ruined it for him. He sat through bad ones right to the end. Uncle Louis was different. He used to say, 'I don't pay to be bored.' He'd walk out of one if it showed any signs of doing that to him.

When a film was over, my father wasn't inclined to talk about it much. He was different from Keith and Hugo that way. They liked acting them out for us. So did Basil.

Keith did impersonations of Humphrey Bogart and James Cagney. Hugo preferred more modern stars like Clint Eastwood and Gregory Peck.

Basil learned off Burt Lancaster's 'I wish to testify about the Feldenstein case' from 'Judgment at Nuremburg.' In some ways he was more like my father than any of us. He had the same build, the same love of audiences. He even learned off many of my father's recitations. In years to come he delivered them to us like my father did, working up the same kind of emotions as him.

When Keith was a baby, my parents treated themselves to a night at the Estoria sometimes while a 'girl' looked after him. For an hour or so they soaked themselves in the never-never land of Hollywood, thinking back to a time when life was a party and the future a long way away.

My father loved spy films. Except he didn't say 'spy,' he said 'espionage.' 'Dr No' came to Ballina in 1962. It was the first James Bond film. Sean Connery was in it. His name was a bit like my mother's maiden name. My father didn't like it. It was too gimmicky for him. He couldn't take it seriously. He preferred the old black and white Cold War films, and gangster ones.

My mother was more interested in family ones. She liked 'The Thin Man' series with William Powell. She pronounced his name 'Po-well' instead of 'Pow-ell' the way the rest of us did. Myrna Loy was with him in them. She had one of those heart-shaped faces so many stars of that era had – Lillian Gish, Claudette Colbert, Jane Wyman and lots of others.

Most of the films he brought me to were ones made in the fifties and sixties. These weren't as interesting to him as the thirties and forties ones he went to with my mother when they were first married, the ones that inspired so much of his fashion sense – the white scarves of Edward G. Robinson, the grey waistcoat, the studs and collars of his shirts, the fob watch, the elbow garter.

If I was lucky enough, an old gangster film would be screened at the Estoria and he'd bring me to it. I'd see the kind of film he would have seen before I was born, the kind he brought my older brothers and sisters to.

This was a world far from the mundanity of Muredach's, a world where every bar had a beautiful 'dame' who doubled as a nightclub singer. A world where cops followed robbers and always came out on top even though your heart was with the robbers.

They may have performed violent deeds but your heart was with them. It was with them even when they drilled bullets into colourless 'heroes.' Their arrogance flew in the face of the obedience we were expected to show at Muredach's.

They gave me a licence to be rebellious even if it was only from the perch of my red velvet cushion in the Estoria. Afterwards I'd revert to my ordinary life, like Superman going back to being Clark Kent in the 'Daily Planet.' I took escapism wherever I got it, for however short a time.

His favourite kinds of thrillers were what he called 'Hitchcocks' - the ones directed by Alfred Hitchcock. They were special because Hitchcock was 'the master of the macabre.' I think he must have seen nearly every film Alfred Hitchcock made. He had a special feeling for 'Vertigo,' having suffered from that condition himself.

He ruined 'Psycho' for me by telling me the plot the night he saw it. I was too young to be allowed into the cinema when it came to Ballina but some of my brothers and sisters did. They said they couldn't sleep for weeks afterwards. It's probably just as well we didn't have showers in those days.

When we weren't going to the pictures we played cards. We whiled away the long nights of winter with Switch and Poker and other games like Newmarket. In the summers we cycled to places like Rosserk or Moyne Abbey or Enniscrone, a beach town eight miles from us.

I felt sorry for him. He hadn't had the experience of growing up with eight siblings. Maybe he didn't even have the experience of growing up with one, being away at boarding school so much.

Uncle Louis was in boarding school too. I never heard him talking about his childhood with Aunt Mary or Aunt Nellie. It was hard to imagine the four of them doing anything together like we did. Maybe that's because I never saw any photographs of the four of them when they were young, either together or apart.

I was a Pisces. If I was away from the sea for any length of time I almost got physically sick. It was probably fated that I'd be born near a beach. The bonus was that it happened to be probably the most beautiful ones in the country.

My father didn't come with us much. When he did it was special. He always looked incongruous sitting in the sand in his suit but it was hard to imagine him any other way. Casual clothes were never for him. He'd have looked ridiculous in bathing togs. I imagined if he went in swimming it would have been in his suit.

He worried about the rest of us going in. Our cousin Charlie, the son of my mother's sister Florence, almost drowned one year at the pier. Another year a local boy chased a beach ball into a whirlpool and lost his life. I never learned to swim so I didn't go out far. My father said that even if you were a good swimmer you could get cramp or be caught by a change in the tides. 'Always swim parallel to the shore,' he said, 'and don't swim after a meal.'

Modern fathers play with their children on beaches. Ours didn't. It was enough that he was there with us. Some days he'd be quiet. There would be a faraway look in his eyes as he gazed out at the sea. If my mother was with us I'd ask her why he wasn't talking to us. She'd just say, 'He's stressed with work.'

Sometimes I'd see him poring over a file in his office. It was probably the same as the way he pored over his examination papers in Trinity years before. I'd feel sorry for him as I saw the worry lines on his face.

He wasn't like his father. I didn't want him to be. All any of us could do was be ourselves. If his father had been in Trinity maybe he'd have been sucked into the party lifestyle too. It's too easy to judge someone from the outside. What we never had we never miss.

It saddened me to see him trying to get himself ready for his next appearance in the courthouse. The Roaring Twenties were over. This was real life. A dull file had to be prepared for an even duller case so he could fulfil the role of husband and father for his growing brood.

Norfolk

My parents and Clive at his ordination

Money

Ballina had only 6000 people in it. Many of my father's cases were small. Few enough of them made much money for him. Someone might be arrested for not having a light on their bicycle or for begging outside the bishop's palace. There wasn't much crime in Ballina then.

I remember our local guard coming in to Muredach's one day. That was the college we all went to. He was there to give us a lecture on road safety. He spoke about a woman he saw on a bicycle who tied a scarf around her head while she was cycling, taking her hands off the bars to do so. It was as if it was the most shocking thing in the world. We were a long way from having a murder in the town, something that would eventually happen.

My father had a lot of his defendants' offences quashed by the Probation Act. 'Every dog is entitled to his first bite,' he'd say to judges. The people he got off would be delighted but he was always worried about people in this situation. They were vulnerable. 'Someone could put a bullet up their behind,' he said, 'and claim provocation.' They were walking round with a 'sword of Damocles' over their heads. He told me a story of a man who was walking down the street one day when he felt himself being prodded from behind. He didn't look around out of fear. It was only when he got to the end of the street that he realised it was a goat that was prodding him.

If he got a house sale it was good money for little enough work. Other cases were more difficult. He hated anything technical like evidence to do with car accidents or skid marks or anything like that. It wasn't the way his brain worked. He was better if a case had a personal angle, something he could get his teeth into in court.

Some days he'd be in 'powerful' form, to use my mother's word. A case would finish and he'd have performed well in it. The money from it would be enough to pay any bill that was outstanding and leave enough over for a night out with my mother or with friends. He'd gather us all around him like the Von Trapp family and entertain us with some childish charade and we'd think it was always going to be like that, but then he'd have his bad days when cases went wrong and he'd say to my mother, 'It isn't working out, Pat.'

She'd do her best to tell him there were bad times before and that they'd passed. She'd say there was no point worrying because it didn't change anything. Her common sense was the opposite of his idea of life as a feast or a famine. When he was in his cups the bad thoughts came. She'd have her work cut out for her trying to get him back to himself. Then one day something would happen that brought him back, a windfall or a word of praise from someone to bring a smile to his face.

Money drifted in and out. He seemed to spend it as soon as it came in. His accounts were like a leaky bucket. No matter how much he earned there seemed to be more demanded for food, clothes, electricity, all the things every family had to pay. The difference with our one was that it was multiplied by nine.

There was also the problem of clients who didn't pay up on time. He said to a man once, 'Don't worry about what you owe me.' The man said, 'Thank you.' My father then said, 'There's no point in the two of us worrying about it!' He hated chasing after people for debts. It wasn't in his nature.

The other people in his family had it easier. Uncle Louis was earning good money as a doctor. Aunt Nellie had a modest lifestyle so she didn't need too much. Aunt Mary was married to one of the richest people in the town.

Every now and then I heard my father and mother talking about money in their room. They stopped if I went into it.

She worried more about it than he did. He seemed to be able to put it to the back of his mind.

Maybe he did that because he couldn't cope with all the things it entailed. Trinity had inculcated an escapist attitude into him that he found difficult to shake off. If he was in a bar or at a function he got carried away with the atmosphere to the exclusion of everything else.

He liked having my mother with him at these events but she'd have preferred to stay at home with us. She never went for anything flashy. Even the fur coat he bought for her didn't look right on her. He'd like to have bought her more things like that but she didn't want them. If she was the type of woman who did she wouldn't have married him in the first place.

At Christmas he bought us expensive presents from Benny Walkin's shop down by the Moy. I remember getting Scalextric one year. It was exciting but it broke after a few days. That was the problem with elaborate toys. They often broke. You were often better off with something more old-fashioned. Hugo and Basil played with Meccano sets. I inherited its modern equivalent, Lego.

Simple presents were the best. A bike with gears or something like that. I was fascinated by the dynamo on Hugo's one, watching it lighting up on the dark nights as he set off for the swimming pool down by Bunree.

We often got bored with elaborate presents. My mother said we had more fun with the boxes they came in. She'd see us running round the back yard with the boxes over our head pretending we were King Arthur or the Knights of the Round Table. When I look back on these years now it's with a special fondness.

None of us were beaten. We were never sent to our room. We were never grounded. That didn't mean we didn't argue. My mother said she listened to us going hammer and tongs at one another about a penny sometimes when we played cards for money. The next day she'd find it under the table. The point was that it didn't matter. The argument did.

It was the same with my father. He'd have discussions about politics with his friends in the bars and none of them would be resolved. It would be just people in love with the sound of their own voices or the drink talking. 'Nobody ever went out of a room,' he said to me once, 'with a different viewpoint than they came into it with.' He liked to quote Thomas Paine's dictum, 'A man convinced against his will/Is of the same opinion still.'

He usually got wrapped up in it all. Arguments about Padraic Pearse or James Connolly or Charles Stewart Parnell, the 'uncrowned king of Ireland.' Questions about Parnell never stopped. Why did the country turn against him? Was he unfairly treated for his relationship with Kitty O'Shea?

Eamon De Valera was another familiar subject. People always got hot under the collar about Dev, the so-called 'Spanish onion in the Irish stew.' If he hadn't had a foreign connection he'd probably have been executed after the 1916 rising. He was a romantic figure then but in my time he wasn't. the longer he lived, the more he personified everything that was drab about Ireland. Should he have sent Michael Collins to London in 1922 to try and negotiate with the Brits about the 32 counties or gone himself?

Such arguments never had resolutions. Maybe they were more interesting because of that. 'It was better than personal talk,' he said, 'The discussions were like shields to prevent us from backbiting one another.'

They would go on into the small hours in the bars. Many of these had secret after hours 'arrangements.' Some of these were even in collusion with the guards. If I was up late for some reason or if I was walking by the street outside the bars I'd hear whispering going on.

Getting ready for a dinner dance

The voices would go quiet when I passed, then start rising again.

When the bars eventually closed down their shutters, the discussions would continue onto the street outside, more loudly now. Often I'd hear shouting from my room. Now and again a punch might be thrown. If it was bad enough it would get into the 'Western.' My father might be a witness to it. He might even be called on to defend the person who threw it.

He'd tell my mother about the night's events when he came home, dramatizing them like one of his recitations or a film he might have seen in the Estoria. Both of them would be aware that not much happened in the town so when something did it had to be exaggerated.

He'd go into detail with her about everything that happened and she'd try to stay awake listening to him. She wouldn't be as interested in the stories as the fact that he was home safe and sound because that was her priority and what she would have been worried about as the night went after midnight.

I'd hear the two of them going up to their bedroom afterwards and then the house would be quiet. All you'd hear would be the music from the Town Hall if there was a dance on there or maybe the sound of someone kicking a can down the street if there wasn't. Eventually I'd edge towards sleep.

The next morning I'd ask my father what the discussions were about. Sometimes he'd have forgotten. If he remembered he might say it didn't matter. It was 'inconsequential.'

The atmosphere was gone now. The people he was drinking with were back in their homes. Tomorrow their lives would be the same as they were before the night began. The Civil War would still have ended the way it did and the same people would be in power.

My father (centre) with two friends

The world would continue to spin. The 1916 heroes would still have been assassinated. Parnell would still have been martyred by his own people and so would Michael Collins.

Collins would still have come back from London with only 26 counties instead of 32.

Nobody's opinion would have changed.

People would just be left with their hangovers.

They'd continue to say what they always said and their friends would pretend to listen to them.

And the penny would still be under the table.

Departures

Keith and Clive did the Leaving Cert in 1955. They left Ballina afterwards. Keith went to UCD to do a B. Comm. For some reason he did a B.A. at the same time. I never knew why. I'm not sure he did either. He stayed with my Aunt Florence, my mother's sister. She ran a guest house in Dun Laoghaire.

Clive entered the Jesuits, going to a place in Emo for his induction. My father was proud of him. He looked on the Jesuits as the 'aristocracy' of the church.

My mother was broken-hearted when Clive left home. He said he wanted to go on the Missions. She knew that meant years abroad without being allowed home. He had his sights set on Northern Rhodesia. Edward Murphy entered the Jesuits that year too. He would eventually go to Zimbabwe, not too far away from Clive in Africa.

June and Ruth were the next to go. That was a few years later. June got a job in the Irish Permanent Building Society in O'Connell Street in Dublin. Ruth started working in the American Embassy in Ballsbridge. They came home at Easter and Christmas and any other time they had a few days off.

They had busy social lives. June had a lot of boyfriends. It was difficult fending them off. My father had a solicitor's clerk working with him in Ballina called Vincent Troy. He was interested in June that way but she had too much going on in Dublin.

Vincent was always up and down to the house on the pretext of some job or other so he could see her. I felt sorry for him. I think he was a good bit older than her. His hair was going thin. He was the first man I ever saw with a hairpiece.

My mother in her riding gear

Northern Rhodesia got its independence in 1964 after over 70 years of British rule. Afterwards it became Zambia. It had a black president, Kenneth Kaunda. Clive went there after being in Emo. As well as being a religious instructor he taught soccer to Kaunda's son.

Hugo and Basil left Ballina that year. They were in the same class in Muredach's. Hugo had a big interest in drama. He used to put on plays using people from the street. One of them was based on the film 'West Side Story.' It came to the Estoria in 1962.

I was too small to see the screen properly in those days. A red velvet cushion used to be put under me to lift me up. I felt special having it brought out for me every time I went up the stairs.

Basil was sociable. He was out of the house a lot seeing his friends. He was also very devout. There were pictures of saints like Dominic Savio and Gerard Majella on the walls. He was particularly devoted to these. Everyone thought he was going to be a priest. One day when he was cycling down to Enniscrone with Hugo he said, 'I have something to tell you. I'm not going into the priesthood.' Hugo said back to him, 'I have something to tell you. I am.'

He entered All Hallows seminary in 1964. Basil followed Keith into UCD. He studied Engineering there. He didn't have to go to Aunt Florence like Keith did. Keith was now renting a flat in Phibsboro. Basil joined him in it. Ruth was there too. June was in one in Haddington Road.

My father was sad to see the house thinning out. There were only three of us left now.

It didn't suit me that Hugo and Basil were gone from Muredach's. I was the only boy in the family who was there on my own. I just missed being with them by a year. Why wasn't I the oldest member of the family, I wondered, instead of the youngest? If I was Keith I'd have had Clive there with me. If I was Hugo I'd have had Basil. I left

Norfolk at 9.15. every morning and cycled down to a place where they drummed boring poems into my head that I was expected to repeat like shopping lists to people stood before me with canes in their hands and expressions on their faces that suggested they'd never lived.

One of the teachers had a 'set' on me. Some of the others referred to me as 'Malone' instead of 'Dillon-Malone.' Maybe that was to pull me down. If that was their reason they did me a favour as I never liked the double-barrel name anyway.

My father wanted us all to be conscious of our status even if he couldn't afford to send us to boarding schools. Most of us wouldn't have wanted to go to them anyway. It was different for him or my mother. She'd boarded in The Bower. That was in a time where parents were more distant from their children. The wrench of parting was less. We were more cossetted. There was a suggestion Audrey and Jacinta would go to The Bower at one stage but I don't think it would have suited them.

He gave out to us about the 'nouveau riches' who were sending their children to such places. 'Even if we haven't a bob we're superior to those people,' he'd say. Maybe that was true but what good was blue blood if you couldn't back it up?

'Money is the new class,' he said. I couldn't see what was wrong with that. If they had the money weren't they entitled to spend it any way they like? On the other end of the scale, what good was breeding if you couldn't back it up? 'Don't give out to me about the fact that we came down in the world,' he said. I said I wasn't giving out to him. I was happier to be as we were instead of living in some boring mansion with servants where you were afraid to touch anything in case you scratched it.

I thought of his comments about 'The Brolly Brigade,' about the putdowns of my grandfather. Maybe he was right about the petty mentalities of small towns. Sean MacDonnell's brother Joe said to me one day in their father's shop on Garden Street, 'It's the penny looking down on the ha'penny.'

I had a knot in my stomach going down to Muredach's every morning. A lot of the teachers were tough. There was a system of corporal punishment in place at the time that they had to adhere to. It was the way things were in most colleges. There was one teacher we had who used to follow us round the classroom to beat us up. After a while it became like a joke, a game of hide and seek.

We were beaten for not knowing our lessons. That meant nothing to a lot of my classmates. They were used to getting hit at home. Some of them used to say, 'If I told my father I got a belt at school he'd give me another one.' The thinking was that you probably deserved it. My father never raised a finger to any of us in Norfolk. From that point of view it was more of a culture shock to be hit at school.

One of the teachers had a set on me. I think he had a problem with me being a solicitor's son. He was a farmer's son and I was the pupil who had to be 'pulled down.' He used to make for me every day, cornering me between two rows of desks and punching me for little or no reason. I knew I could never tell my father about him. He'd have been down to him like a shot.

Sometimes I dreamed about this man, or had nightmares about him. In one of them I was in a chasm and my father was trying to pull me out. I sank farther and farther into it as he reached for me. I always woke up just before I reached the bottom, his hands grasping thin air as I sank away from him.

He didn't encourage me to hit someone back if I was punched by a classmate in the playground but he would have been livid if he knew a teacher hit me. I felt it was more important to stand up for yourself with people of your own age.

I'd have loved it if he encouraged me to box. There was a boxing club above the room where we played snooker in the Hibs. We'd hear them jousting with one another as we played our shots. Sawdust used to come down through the floorboards above us sometimes and settle on the cloth of the table. We'd have to sweep it off or the cue ball would wobble.

I never expected the teachers in Muredach's not to hit us. It was as much a part of their job as writing on the blackboard with chalk. Audrey and Jacinta went to the Convent of Mercy. They said the nuns used sarcasm on them instead of hitting them. That was worse in their opinion. I agreed with them. The man who said 'Sticks and stones can hurt my bones but names will never hurt me' was wrong. Names were often worse.

We got sarcasm in the college too. I remember our Science teacher saying to one of my classmates one day, 'If it was raining, you'd be out with a fork.' It was only years later I saw that was a quotation by Brendan Behan. Not even the wit in Muredach's was original.

Heaven was when we got a day off. I was absent a lot, either through sickness or pretending to be sick. It's probably significant that I'm not in the only photograph I have of my class.

My father let me stay home from school anytime I wanted. My mother was more insistent that I go, maybe fearing that I'd follow in his footsteps from his time in Trinity, letting the grass grow under my feet as the years slid by. His attitude was more like, 'Batten down the hatches and close off the wicked world outside.'

My mother was never someone to say, 'Wait till your father comes home' if we did something wrong but she was less easily won over than him. We could pull the wool over his eyes easily. At the merest hint of a symptom of being unwell he'd hoosh us off to bed. If he saw the need for it he'd ring Dr Igoe, our GP.

The other doctor we had was Aubrey Bourke. He delivered me. I was said to be named after him. It's also possible I was named after the poet Aubrey De Vere. My father was reading a biography of him the night I was born.

Dr Bourke also fathered Ireland's future president, Mary Robinson. Mary was one of the most liberal women ever to come out of Ballina. I don't know what my father would have made of her. He was probably aware of her growing up. Like him she had to get a dispensation to go to Trinity and like him she studied Law there. She graduated a bit quicker than he did, though that's not saying much.

I felt my name attracted too much attention to itself. I never wanted that. Whenever I walked down the street with my father I stayed in his shadow. If people came up to him and started talking to him I wanted to disappear. He was the opposite, taking great delight in showing me off.

'Isn't he shooting up?' he'd say even if I'd only grown half an inch since they last saw me, and they'd have to ooh and aah.

I'd blush and he'd go, 'Take whatever compliments you get,' he'd say, 'It isn't everyone who gives them.'

I couldn't explain to him that I didn't want compliments. I didn't want any kind of attention. I just wanted to be left alone.

Man about town

School

My father usually bought me treats if I was home from school due to sickness. I remember getting a ream of paper from him once. I don't know why. It was hardly for drawing. I couldn't draw a straight line then and still can't. It was hardly for writing either. I remember writing a few lines of a story once on the edge of a Cornflakes packet but nothing else.

A more usual treat was comics. I read the *Beano* and the *Dandy*. Hugo and Basil read *Victor*. June and Ruth read *School Friend* and *Girls Crystal.* Audrey and Jacinta read these comics too, and later *Jackie*. They used to ask me to go down to Brennans shop to get them for them on the day they came out. I always put them inside the *Beano* anytime I did that for fear of being called a sissy.

When I finished reading my comics my father would ask me how I was feeling. 'Do you think you'll be able to go to school tomorrow?' he'd say. A lot of the time I felt he knew I was putting it on. He never minded that. My mother would have.

When I'd get back to Muredach's the teachers would ask me what was wrong with me. I'd usually make up some excuse. Now and then one of them would say, 'I saw you at the pictures last week.' I'd have to say, 'I felt a bit better that night.' They'd never fall for my malingering like my father did.

I wasn't sick most of the days I stayed off school. I was just sick of school. People said to me, 'Why do you do that? You're good at your lessons.' I saw their point. I did fairly well at exams. It was a psychological thing. Just thinking about going down to the college made me nauseous. I woke up with the nausea. It was there as I put up on my clothes, as I had my breakfast, as I got out my bike and cycled down Arthur Street past the wholesale shop with the three green windows. I'll never forget them. They had parts of the word 'Wholesale' on each of them. The first one had 'Who,' the second 'Les' and the third 'Ale.' I never connected them. It's strange what you remember.

I'd turn right at Geraghty's and go down Garden Street, then Bridge Street, then across the bridge towards the Cathedral. The Cathedral and the College were the two big buildings of my youth, the bulwarks of church and state, both intimidating and forming me.

I got hit sometimes for having been out of school. I didn't mind that. It was worse being punished for not knowing your lessons, especially if it was as a result of something being taught badly. That happened in most schools in Ireland when I was growing up. It was just the way things were.

I never told my father anytime I was hit but he'd know by me if I was upset. That usually meant yet another treat, either a comic or film or maybe a trip down the country if he had to see a client in some out of the way place.

Whenever he was going on any kind of long trip he'd order a 'hackney' or 'batman,' to drive him. He usually sat in the back seat unless he really liked him.

There was one taxi driver we employed called Pat Hughes. He was rumoured to be the slowest driver in the country. Apparently he stopped to give a pedestrian a lift one day and the pedestrian refused it saying, 'Sorry, Pat, I'm in a hurry.'

When we got back to Ballina my father would usually be busy working on things to do with who he saw when he was away. Sometimes he let me help him. I'd lick envelopes for him or put blotting paper on pages to let the ink dry into them. I knew he could do these kinds of things himself. He was just making me feel important. He didn't need the envelopes licked as he had a substance he put on them to make them wet.

After he finished his business he'd usually ask me if he could help me with my homework. Sometimes I asked him to do my Latin exercise for me. It was crazy having to learn it when it was a dead language. I asked him for help at Geography too as I had a blind spot at that. History was another one of the subjects he liked.

The one thing I never asked him for help at was Irish. He had no interest in it. If any of us was speaking it he'd say, 'Stop that bad language.' I hated Irish too. A lot of that was down to the way it was taught, to the fact that we were hit if we got things wrong in it.

Someone once said that the English beat Irish out of us and the Irish beat it back into us again. It was true. We were never given any liking for it. It was just grammar and memory work and little or no conversation. Audrey and Jacinta had to study most of their subjects through it in the Convent. 'It's a wonder they don't teach English through Irish,' Audrey said.

The main thing my father helped me with in Muredach's was my essays. I hated having to do them. Other subjects weren't too bad when you knew where to go for the answers but with an essay you were called on to use your imagination. I didn't think I had one.

He'd sit me down at the kitchen table and give me pointers. 'You have to be exact in what you say,' he said to me one day, 'A boy I knew got an essay to write once called "A Walk in the Country." He wrote the most beautiful essay about all the sights he saw but he was given no marks because his first sentence was, "I jumped up on my bicycle."'

He corrected my grammar. 'I used to get it wrong myself when I was your age,' he told me. Some words confused him when he was young. He used to pronounce 'bishop' as 'bis-hop' instead of 'bish-op,' for instance. He spelt 'ski-ing' as 'shi-ing' and 'jeep' as 'zeep.'

Once he got over his blind spots he became a stickler for what he called 'The Queen's English.' If one of us was at the door and we said, 'It's me,' he'd say, 'Don't say that. Say 'It is I.' If we were in a shop and ordered rashers he'd say, 'It's not rashers. It's rashers of bacon.' He was adamant that we put the right word in the right place. If someone said, 'You've got your facts wrong,' he'd say, 'Facts are never wrong.' He hated when people said 'Presently' to mean 'At present' rather than its real meaning of 'In the future.'

He loved words. All I had to do was give him the title of the essay I was asked to do and he'd be off. He walked up and down the kitchen floor dictating them to me. His hands would be behind his back. He used to flick the ash of a cigarette he was smoking onto the floor. It became like his ash tray.

He smoked a brand called Boston. They were a bit smaller than the usual cigarettes. He had a silver case that he kept them in. When he flicked a switch, the top popped open. There were always ten cigarettes inside with a little red band over them. When he took one out he always tapped the tip on the case before lighting it.

Boston went off the market early. He smoked a brand called Peter Stuyvesant afterwards. Then Major, then Benson & Hedges Gold Bond, then Players. I can still see the drawing of the bearded sailor on the front of the packet of Players.

There'd usually be a smell of nicotine off his fingers. When he drew on a cigarette he seemed to inhale it down to his toes. He was said to smoke 100 a day.

He never did anything by halves. If he ordered ice cream from Clarkes in King Street it was a whole carton of it rather than a single cone. He'd lower it in record time. My mother knew he had an addictive personality. He was that way in everything he did. She worried about the drink getting a hold of him from that point of view.

One day she told me she didn't think he smoked anything like 100 cigarettes a day. 'Maybe he lit 100,' she said, 'but he probably only smoked a half or a quarter of them.' He'd light one and then forget about it, going into another room to light other ones. She hated that kind of waste.

She was also a smoker herself. As a child in Roscommon she'd picked up butts dropped by her older brothers and smoked them. This was in the era where fake cigarettes were sold to us in sweet shops to get us in on them, an era where your local GP might even offer you one at the end of a consultation to 'relax' you.

It turned out to be the beginning of a lifelong habit for her. She used to give them up for Lent every year. After she'd go back on them she'd throw up after the first one. She sucked Fox's mints during Lent to have something to substitute for them.

Sometimes she followed my father from room to room looking for the missing cigarettes. She thought he was capable of burning the house down if he left one by the curtains or somewhere else that could catch fire. She'd find them everywhere, usually with the ash in the shape of the original cigarette.

Because he was lighting so many, he used a lot of matches. 'Friendly' was written on the boxes. After he was finished a box he'd give it to me. I invented a game where I stood them all up in a circle. When you tipped one they all fell like dominoes.

Sometimes when he was dictating the essays to me I'd be so entranced watching him smoking that I'd forget to write down what he was saying. He'd say, 'Did you get that?' and I wouldn't have. He'd have to repeat it.

He walked as he dictated. His mind seemed to work better when he was moving. He told me a story about a king of Spain who was so small that whenever had had a problem he used to walk up and down under his bed all night to try and think of a solution for it. It was nonsense of course but I believed it. I had this vision of a two foot high member of the royalty. He enjoyed talking about kings. He'd love to have been one.

Even though he liked walking, he wasn't athletic. I couldn't imagine him running anywhere to save his life. He told me a story about a day when he was playing rugby in Castleknock. He froze on the pitch as a forward ran towards the touchline for a try. He was expected to tackle him but he couldn't move. 'Feet, do your duty,' he said, looking downwards. He didn't move, but the forward fell on top of him and his try was averted. 'I got praised for doing nothing,' he said.

I don't remember him ever going to a game of rugby or even watching one on television. He was even less likely to go to a soccer game even though it had English overtones. Rugby was posh but soccer wasn't. As the saying went, rugby was a hooligan's game played by gentlemen whereas soccer was a gentleman's game played by hooligans.

Gaelic football or hurling were even farther down the pecking order. I didn't think he approved of Hugo and Basil going down to Belleek to play soccer. I joined them sometimes. My mother had a completely different attitude. She didn't mind if we all came back 'as black as the ace of Spades,' as she put it.

He used to bring us walking in a place called Primrose Hill. It was near Leigue cemetery where our family vault was. I don't remember these walks but I imagine I was on some of them. Basil wrote a poem about them that captures the magic of the time, describing us as nine ducklings in our Von Trapp style chrysalis.

At night time he did a different kind of walking. He'd go in and out through us as we said the rosary. We'd be kneeling down with our elbows on chairs. He'd thread his way through us.

His hands would still be behind his back but instead of a cigarette in them now there would be a pair of rosary beads as he gave out the various decades. I used to watch his fingers going through the beads waiting for the last 'Hail Mary' before the decade changed in case I might be called on to give one out.

Religion was everywhere in those days. There were processions with the Knights of Columbanus and other organisations. Bunting would be put across the street if someone from the town was ordained. On Mission Sunday, Redemptorists priests would put our hearts crossways telling us what would happen to us if we didn't obey the Ten Commandments.

My father had four uncles who were priests as well as having Clive and Hugo in seminaries. He didn't have much to do with the priests in Muredach's but he loved going up to the convent to see the nuns. He'd put on his best bib and tucker and make his way there, going down Arthur Street and left to Convent Hill, then up past the corkscrew bend at Arthur Wills' house.

It was a novelty for them having a man in the convent. The best china would be brought out to give him tea, and the triangular sandwiches. They danced attendance on him as he told his stories to them. The performer in him would come out. The convent was a stage to him like the courthouse was. He had no problem rising to the occasion.

At home he often quoted verses from the Bible. Sometimes he did so humorously. The one he quoted most often was, 'Whom the Lord loveth, he chastiseth.' 'If that's the case,' he said, 'I think I'll just bid him "Good day" from the other side of the street.' It was like the way he said he loved Aunt Nellie from a distance.

He told another joke about a man who went to confession one day and said he'd had 'bad thoughts.' The priests asked him if he'd 'entertained' them. 'No, Father,' the man replied, 'but they sure entertained me!'

There were always priests coming to the house. They'd get the royal treatment. My father would take out the decanter for them. You'd nearly step off the pavement onto the road if one passed you on the street. I remember one of them stuffing a £1 note down my neck once. I think his name was Father Munnelly.

My father's attitude to religion changed when Pope John the 23rd entered the Vatican. 'He's too liberal,' he said. He felt his policies affected the priests in Ireland. 'They don't know how to run parishes anymore,' he complained.

If he went to Confession he felt he wasn't given enough penance. 'Religion is all 'kindness to the cat' since Vatican II came in,' he said, 'There was a time Rome spoke. Now it just whispers.' He thought it was acceding to Pope John's agenda in a desperate attempt to hold onto its adherents. Nuns were 'jumping the wildcat' up and down the aisles of churches. There was a series on television that had one riding a motorcycle. He turned the set off anytime he saw it. He didn't even like Clive going around in 'mufti,' as he called it.

In his world you were one thing or another. Black was black and white was white. Ne'er the twain should meet. When he confessed a sin to a priest he wanted him to say something like, 'If thine eye offends thee, pluck it out.' He wanted him to be like the fire-and-brimstone preachers.

Even though he had problems with the way the church was run, its straightforward theology of sin and redemption appealed to him. He knew when he hadn't lived up to his expectations of himself and never tried to sugarcoat it. He was good at saying, 'Mea culpa.' 'Even Jesus fell three times,' he'd say.

In another mood he was capable of telling jokes about these things. 'They say there'll be weeping and gnashing of teeth in hell,' he said to me one day, 'What about all the people with dentures?'

He was a devotee of a man called Cardinal Lefebvre. Lefebvre campaigned for the retention of the Tridentine Mass. My father preferred it when the priest had his back to him in the cathedral.

He liked the Latin as well. He'd learned a lot of it for his Law degree. He was always using Latin phrases like 'ipso facto' or 'infra dig.' I didn't know what most of them meant. 'Infra dig' I heard as 'In for a dig,' meaning 'lined up for a punch.' At Mass I parroted other Latin phrases like 'Et cum spiritu tuo' without knowing what they meant either.

He told me once that he'd like to have been a priest. The idea of giving sermons appealed to the performer in him. 'Whenever I hear one about hellfire and damnation,' he said, 'Everyone looks at the person in the pew opposite them as if he's talking about them. They don't see the mote in their own eye. I'd put an end to that if I was in the pulpit.'

Sometimes I thought he wanted me to be a priest too. It put a burden on me because I was never inclined that way. Religion was a tense experience for me growing up.

I thought I'd committed a mortal sin if the Communion wafer touched my teeth at Mass. The way the priests taught Catechism inculcated these kinds of fears in us. They said faith was a gift but if you didn't have it you'd go to hell. It seemed like a contradiction. If you had bad thoughts and you went to Communion afterwards that was a mortal sin too, but if you didn't go to Communion you could go to hell as a result of not having God inside you. It was another contradiction.

My father told me not to worry about things like that. He told me not to worry about school either. Sometimes I told him I hated going down to Muredach's. He said he'd take me out of it if I wanted. I knew that could never happen. Where would I go? We didn't have the money for boarding schools.

I often thought I'd like to go to the 'Tech' to study something practical. Books were fine but as the saying went, they couldn't butter parsnips. A lot of the people I knew from The Hibernian Hall went there. That was a snooker hall near us. We called it The Hibs for short. When they talked about things like carpentry and other trades it sounded exciting to me. They couldn't understand that. To them the subjects I was studying sounded exciting. We all loved our opposites.

The Hibs became like a second home to me over time. In that it was like the Estoria. The difference was that all the family went to the Estoria. The Hibs was my discovery. No other member of the family played snooker. Maybe that was part of its appeal for me.

I adopted the tastes of the rest of the family in things like music. In films I was a 'chip off the old block,' going to gangster films that my father liked. Spending time in the Hibs was the first part of my growing up, of growing away from my roots.

He didn't like me being there. He knew most of the people I'd be meeting would be from 'the wrong side of the tracks' as he put it. Many of them were poor. I told him I relaxed more with poor people than rich ones.

'Don't go against your background,' he said to me.

I wanted to tell him I didn't want to be like him or like my mother. I didn't want to have a double-barrelled name or come from a county family. I didn't want to ride to the hounds or hob-nob with the bourgeoisie. All I wanted to do was get from one end of the day to the other without tension in my life.

Maybe doing the essays for me was his way of holding onto me, of keeping me away from people who'd give me different priorities. He didn't want me talking about carpentry. That was for tradesmen, for people who came in the back door of Norfolk instead of the front one.

I remember getting an essay once called 'Our Sweetest Songs Are Those that Tell of Saddest Thought.' I hadn't a clue what it meant but he seemed to be inspired by it.

The essay he wrote for me was probably of third level standard. I don't think the teacher believed I wrote it but he still read it out in class. I was glad it was him and not me. I wouldn't have been able to pronounce half the words.

My father had an exaggerated view of my abilities. If I did well in an exam he'd tap me on the head and say, 'And still they gazed, and still the wonder grew, that one small head could carry all he knew.' It was a quote from Oliver Goldsmith.

Maybe I'd have been more content in Muredach's if Hugo and Basil were there with me. If Audrey and Jacinta were boys they'd have been there. Most of the family besides me had brothers or sisters close to them in age. The three years between myself and Jacinta seemed much more than that to me.

In 1964 I got an extra sister of sorts when our cousin Ann O'Grady came to live with us. She was from a farm in Roscommon near Raheen. We were only six weeks apart in age. Ann went to the Convent of Mercy with Audrey and Jacinta. She became a part of the family immediately.

We used to go down to Bohernasup together to babysit the children of Jimmy Murphy, the youngest of Uncle Eddie's sons. There were two boys, Shane and David. Others arrived later. Ann had a passion for pickled onions. She used to raid the fridge for them.

Jimmy reminded me of my father in ways. Both of them had mercurial personalities. He was very brave. One time he rescued a man from drowning down by the Quay.

The main difference between them was I could never imagine my father driving a car. He'd have got too confused wondering what all those strange things like gear sticks and accelerators were. And how would he ever remember to buy petrol? He'd have expected it to run on fresh air.

Jimmy drove like a Formula One driver. My heart would be in my mouth as he brought us home from the babysitting, especially when he made the turn from Bohernasup onto the Killala Road. It was a hairpin bend he took at such speed he would have made Ayrton Senna looked like a slowcoach.

He died young like that other Jimmy who loved speeding in cars, the film star Jimmy Dean, but it wasn't in a car accident. It was from cancer, the disease that took many of his family so cruelly, including my Aunt Mary, a death my father found it so difficult to recover from.

Yours –
Hugh.

Growing

Ann and myself got up to all sorts of pranks together in Norfolk. One day we decided to drop steel trays out the window of the boxroom to give the people passing by a fright. We certainly succeeded in that. The sound they made would have wakened the dead.

Another time we brought a spool of thread onto the street and wound it out tautly, standing on opposite sides of the road as cars drove into it and broke it.

Ann's mother felt she'd get a better education in Ballina than in Roscommon. The school was small there and the teaching not up to much. She was right. Ann went ahead in leaps and bounds in the convent, eventually getting a scholarship to a school in Belmullet. That was a village at the outermost tip of Mayo. It was said that on a clear day you could see the Statue of Liberty. Why not? It was only 3000 miles away.

Aunt Mary got cancer not long after Ann came to the town. It caused her fragile build to become even more fragile. Cancer was like a death sentence in those days. People were almost as afraid of the word as the disease. It was mostly whispered.

He walked down to Bunree with my mother to visit her many nights. They were always quiet when they got home. She died soon after her diagnosis. He was distraught. 'They say it's harder for a rich person to enter heaven than a camel to go through the eye of a needle,' he said, 'but she would have gone through it flying.'

Uncle Eddie never recovered from her death. They were very devoted to one another. He'd always been a big man. He once told my father he'd give up all his wealth if he could lose weight. Now it fell off. He stopped eating and six months later he was in his grave as well. Paddy, his son, took over the running of the mill. Eddie's daughter, Feena, was my godmother. She was kind to me, sending me a gift every birthday until I was 21.

Two years after Aunt Mary died we had the 50th anniversary of the 1916 rising. To commemorate it, many street names in the town were changed to the names of national heroes. Arthur Street became Teeling Street, though my father still continued to refer to it as Arthur Street. He was stubborn that way. His attitudes would be called right wing today. I didn't think of things like right wing or left wing in those days.

He got very worked up sometimes, telling us authority was breaking down in the church, in society, in politics. It was even breaking down in the law, his own field. The removal of capital punishment, he believed, meant murderers had less to fear now if they were caught. He talked about Albert Pierrepoint, a man who hanged over 600 people in his 'career,' if such it could be called. 'That little piece of rope dangling in the air,' he said, 'kept a lot of us alive.'

Criminals were getting soft treatment nowadays in his view. They'd recruit some quack psychologist to say they hit their head off a stone when they were young. They were seen as mentally unbalanced and got little more than a slap on the wrist when they faced the courts.

'They spend their time watching television in prison,' he'd say. He showed me an article in the paper one day about a dog who bit a man in America. He was judged to be suffering from depression at the time. 'The world is gone to blazes,' he said.

Some criminals excited him in how they eluded the law. He talked about Harvey Crippen, the homeopath who killed his wife in 1910. 'He'd have got away with it if he didn't abscond,' he said. It was almost like he wanted him to.

Another killer he liked talking about was John Christie. Christie was a serial killer who was caught the month I was born in 1953. One of his victims was called Maloney. Just before he was hanged he told Pierrepoint his nose was itchy. Pierrepoint replied, 'It won't bother you for long.'

He also became excited about things like the kidnapping of the Lindbergh baby. It was in the news for many years in the thirties, a bit like O.J. Simpson in our own era.

More than anything he got excited about Hitler, a man who was able to command audiences like a God. 'Was he mad or bad?' he'd say. He knew how close the Nazis came to taking over the world. His life, in many ways, had been dominated by him. He watched him rampaging across Europe throughout the forties. When I asked him what he thought motivated him he said, 'The devil himself doesn't know the mind of man.'

He gave out about what he called 'the rising tide of communism.' A few years earlier the Bay of Pigs incident had taken place. He thought we were all going to be wiped out by the Russians at the time. I did too. I was only eight but I still remember it. It gave me a terror of Russia, a terror I carried with me through my teenage years. When someone told me they went to Moscow once I said to them, 'How did you get back in one piece?' I thought a trip to that country would inevitably be a one-way one. You'd either be murdered or sent to the salt mines of Siberia.

My father used Karl Marx' expression 'dictatorship of the proletariat' if he was talking about the way the working class was thriving. It was like the words of the Rude Boys song, 'The working class can kiss my arse/I've got the foreman's job at last.'

We got a job done on the bathroom once. The plumber charged a fortune for it. It was only a few minutes work. He was aghast. 'Jack's as good as his master today,' he said, 'The poachers have become gamekeepers.'

All eleven of us

Maybe this started in England. One of our teachers in Muredach's used to say, 'When England sneezes, Ireland reaches for its handkerchief.' That was certainly true of the class war.

About a decade before my father said these words, England produced films like *Room at the Top, Saturday Night and Sunday Morning, A Kind of Loving , Look Back in Anger, This Sporting Life.*

They featured the rise of the working class as they poked fun at anachronistic Lord Ha-Ha types living in baronial mansions.I didn't see these kinds of films in Ballina. They were hardly the type of things my father would have brought me to. I doubt Keith would have gone to them either.

Both Keith and my father were more interested in Hollywood's Dream Factory, Keith to escape the drabness of ordinary life and my father to see mirror images of his exalted images of himself on celluloid, a PJ Malone for the next generation.

A lot of his jokes revolved round class. One day he told me one about a cleaning woman in a mansion. The lady of the manor said to her, 'Molly, I could write my name on this piano.' She was referring to the dust on it. Molly said, 'Gee, ma'am, it must be great to be educated.'

He dropped his snobbish attitudes when he drank. Another person came out, someone truer to his real self. 'In vino veritas,' as they say.

Sometimes he became confused with drink. Because he was the person I looked up to so much, I couldn't understand that. The man who knew everything about the law, about English literature and politics and religion and everything else, seemed suddenly dazed by life as he sat at a bar counter. He'd talk about money problems or about how his father never got the credit he deserved in Ballina. He'd look at me pleadingly, wanting me to understand how he was feeling, and I'd want to put my arms round him.

Most people who drink more than was good for them think: I'll pay for this in the morning. My father was too romantic for that. He lost himself in the worlds of the bars, imagining they'd solve all his problems.

I don't ever remember him drinking in the house. It was the atmosphere of these places that excited him. They were his homes from home even though he loved his home. That was his contradiction. My mother didn't mind him being in them as long as he stayed away from 'the hard stuff.' If he had whiskey it changed him. 'It was like a match to a flame' was the way she put it.

The next morning he'd be back to himself again. It would be as if the night never happened. He'd help me with my essays or whatever else I asked him and I'd forget about the person who found life so difficult.

Sometimes he got merry with drink. If that was the case he might even sing a 'camáille.' That was something that would normally have been unthinkable for him.

I remember one of them. It was called 'The Maid of the Sweet Brown Knowe. It went like this:

'Come all you lads and lassies and listen to me a while.

I'll sing for you a verse or two that will cause you all to smile.

It's about a young man I'm going to tell you now.

Who lately went a-courting with the maid of the sweet brown knowe.'

He made jokes about these kinds of songs, saying things like 'The first 34 verses are the best.' It sounded like another putdown of Ireland but behind it all I think he had a soft spot for songs like that.

Another one he liked was 'I'm shy Mary Ellen I'm shy.' Maybe that was because of his mother's name.

There was another song he sang that I didn't know the name of. It had the lines 'He hit her with a feather duster and she fell to the ground/And he wrote to his old fella to send him a -.'

We always expected him to say 'pound' to complete the rhyme but for some reason he always stopped and then said 'quid' with a big smile on his face. I never knew why. Or he might even say 'guinea.' He was always talking about guineas. He said people in posh careers often charged that in fees. I wondered if Uncle Louis did.

Watching him singing songs like that made my father into a much more complicated person. He didn't just sing them. He really got into them. If he sang 'The Maid of the Sweet Brown Knowe' after 'The Green Eye' it sounded strange, almost as strange as my mother singing Bobby Darin's 'Things' – because she found it 'catchy' - after 'Jerusalem.' How could someone go from a hymn to a pop song or from a recitation to a *camáille*?

Both of them had that kind of versatility. I didn't see it in other parents in our street, or any street in the town.

Letters

My father sometimes wrote letters to people who bothered him. He'd tap out his anger on a typewriter, banging on the keys with his index fingers. He typed so fast, sometimes a letter would appear higher than the other ones on the page. If he made a mistake he put loads of Xs across the word. That was the Tipp Ex of the time.

He often typed so loud it sounded like a factory machine. In those days you had to be as strong as Arnold Schwarzenegger to make an imprint on a page. I loved listening to his pounding, to the ping of the machine as he came to the end of a line. He used ribbons that were half red and half black.

He usually put in a sheet of carbon paper behind the sheet he was typing on and another sheet of paper behind that so he'd have a copy of what he wrote in case it got lost. He hit the keys so hard, often the carbon would have holes in it on every second word. I fished them out of his waste paper basket sometimes and held them up to the light to see them properly.

He often had a cigarette in his mouth as he typed. The ash would fall on the floor with the force of his typing, the carpet as ever being his ash tray.

When he had the letters finished I'd usually be asked to post them. My mother would know he didn't really mean what he said in them so she'd tell me not to. The next morning, more often than not, he'd say, 'I wish I hadn't written that letter.' At which point I'd 'discover' it in my pocket and say I'd forgotten to post it. He'd take it from me and tear it up.

Exactly what pressing business I'd have at the dead of night to make me forget to post a letter was something he never enquired about. It also surprised me that he didn't post the letters himself. There was a letterbox outside our door. Maybe subconsciously he didn't want to.

In the daytime I delivered letters from him to other people. They were mainly solicitors he was doing business with. Sometimes they contained what he called 'judicature paper.' I could never pronounce that word properly.

They might have a wax seal on them if they were Grants of Probate. He burned this onto the last page of the documents he was sending. Then he'd put them into huge rectangular envelopes that he was careful to lick to that they stayed sealed. I delivered them to solicitors he was doing business with - Mr Gilvarry, Mr Corr, Bourke Carrig and Loftus and others. There were four clients of his that I remember because of the similarity of their names: Fottrell, Cottrell, Fox and Cox. Cottrell, of course, was also the name of our friends living across the road from us who went back to England in the mid-sixties.

If he was writing a personal letter he used smaller white envelopes with flaps at the back shaped like a V. When he licked these he usually only gave them a cursory lick at the V. After he gave them to me I'd lick them all the way along the sticky part to make sure they stayed shut.

He always gave me some money after I posted them for him. 'Don't spend it all in the one shop,' he'd say. Now and again I got a 1 note from him, one of the ones with Lady Lavery on it in that lovely thick green.

It felt like a million. I didn't want to spend it, just look at it. More usually it would be a smaller amount I'd get, a sixpence or a threepenny bit, one of the bronze-like ones that were twelve-sided. I remember getting a half crown once too, or a half dollar as Keith called it.

One day he gave me a penny with the date 1961 on it. I was fascinated by the fact that it was the same when I turned it upside down. It was like 'PJ Malone JP.' He told me that was a palindrome. I said, 'What's a palindrome'?' He said, 'Able was I ere I saw Elba,'

I didn't know what he was talking about. He said, 'It's the same back to front. Napoleon was supposed to have said something like that when he went into exile.' I didn't know who Napoleon was. I had a vague feeling he was one of his beloved authority figures.

He showed me his legal files sometimes. They were usually written in illegible scripts with lots of Latin phrases. I didn't know how he could understand them. He said he didn't have to. 'You have to look the part in court,' he said, 'even if you could write what you have to say on the back of a stamp.'

His brief case would be bulging with files as he went up to the courthouse. 'I mightn't even look at any of them,' he said, 'Most rulings boil down to what witnesses say. That changes everything. If someone breaks down, you have an open-and-shut case.'

I asked him once if he'd defend a man on a murder charge if he felt he was guilty. 'I wouldn't want to have to,' he said. 'I'd ask him if he was innocent and if he said he was I'd have to go along with that even if I had suspicions about him. If someone told me flat out that he was guilty, obviously I couldn't defend him.'

He was a different man in court than at home. The performer in him took over. It was as if someone pulled a switch. Then the case would end and he'd be my father again.

If none of us were there with him my mother would be nervous wondering how he'd got on. She'd wait to hear his key in the door. If he won you'd know immediately. If he didn't he'd go quiet.

Sometimes there could be a deferral, or what he called mediation. 'A lot of it is red tape,' he used to say, 'The judge gives some kind of direction and a few weeks later

I'm up before him again with the same defendant.' Some decisions seemed to be based on how someone looked or dressed. 'The law is an ass,' he used to say, 'It's all about image. I'm playing a part and they are too.'

He loved talking about the fact that Daniel O'Connell drove 'a coach and four' through almost every Act of Parliament. Most people saw him as a pillar of the establishment but I always felt there was a Guy Fawkes in there somewhere too, or a Samson, delighting in pulling down the pillars of the temple.

I often got money from him if he won a big case. If he gave me a shilling I used it for playing snooker. You got half an hour in the Hibs for that.

I started playing snooker there in 1966. I was thirteen at the time and just about tall enough to reach the table. Up until then I wasn't. He was relieved that I was 'shooting up,' as he put it. I heard from somewhere once that he was so worried about me not growing that he wrote to a doctor in Switzerland to ask him if he could help. I thought that was a bit extreme.

He told me he still had problems with me going to The Hibs. 'You'll only meet the riff-raff there,' he'd say, 'Blackguards who spend their time measuring one another spits at Moylett's corner.'

He wanted me to play in the Moy Club instead. That was a posher club. You'd see these duffers through the window making a big deal out of every shot, old school tie types dolled up to the nines.

They played billiards sometimes as well. It bored me to tears watching them nursing their cannons for hours on end. I could have joined them if I wanted but I had no interest. He'd probably have gone there himself if he liked billiards. The dressing up would have suited him.

The Moy Club had only one table. The Hibs had two. It also had lots more atmosphere. Some of the people who did odd jobs for him played there.

They came from Lord Edward Street, a part of Ballina we called Guntown. They lived in two-up two-down council houses. I liked most of them. You didn't have to watch your words with them like you had to with some of our more well-heeled connections. Many of them couldn't pronounce my name. They called me Audie instead, like Audie Murphy, one of the cowboy stars from films I saw in the Estoria.

Sometimes I went there with a friend from across the road. He used to come up to Norfolk every now and then. We played records on a turntable Aunt Mary gave us. He played the guitar himself. I tried to but I never got good at it.

Other times Sean MacDonnell would come with me. I played so much I had to be scraped off the table. My hands would be aching as I went home. I'd walk down Bury Street thinking of the good shots I got and the ones I should have but didn't, and how I might improve myself the next time.

The people from 'Guntown' called me the Olympic Player. The Olympic Games were taking place in Mexico that year.

'We hear you're going to Mehico,' they'd say to me, pronouncing the word the way the Mexicans themselves did.

Sometimes they added, 'We'll expect you to come back with gold.'

My father and June at Enniscrone

Clive blessing our cousins the O'Gradys

Office

My father's office burned down in 1966. It was a big blow for him. Nothing important was destroyed but the building was too badly damaged for him to work there anymore.

He brought his files back to Norfolk and continued his practice from the house. I couldn't believe how many he had as I didn't go to Bridge Street much. He put a plaque on the wall outside the door. It said, 'Hugh Dillon-Malone, Commissioner for Oaths.' When I saw it first I thought it was something to do with farming.

His new office was in the dining-room of the house. It was where he used to keep all his novels up to now. It had a mahogany table in it that we used to eat on at Christmas or special occasions. We put an embroidered white cloth on it. Christmas presents were also stored there on Christmas Eve. I found them one year. It was the year I discovered to my horror that 'There ain't no Sanity Clause,' as Groucho Marx put it. All the presents were on the table. They came from the International Stores, not Lapland.

I knew that because I'd seen them on the window the week before. It was a shop that was owned by a man called Benny Walkin. He was one of my father's clients. Sometimes instead of paying him a fee he'd give him toys for us. It was another 'Contra' arrangement like the one with Paddy Mulligan. I thought of it almost like barter.

There was no cloth on the dining-room table now, just his files. Sometimes he let us play table tennis on it. We took them off and put them on shelves that were on the walls until we were finished. Clive built us another table afterwards. He was good at carpentry.

The table in the dining room had flaps on it that extended its length. If a ball landed on the part of the table where the flap was it gave a strange bounce. Sometimes I aimed for that part deliberately to gain an advantage. It worked the other way as well. If the ball bounced straight up in the air it gave the other player a chance for a 'slam dunk' shot like in tennis.

The balls were always breaking on us. My father said they must have been made with a fault. Today we'd call it built-in obsolescence. 'They do that to keep you buying more of them,' he said. 'If someone made one that didn't burst he'd be sacked.'

Work was more casual for him in Norfolk than in Bridge Street. Some days he didn't even dress, seeing people in his dressing gown instead. If they were giving an oath he'd ask them to put their hand on a Bible.

After he was finished his business with them he'd spend ages talking to them, pinning them to the wall with some story or other. He came to life at times like that. It was as if he was still the Trinity student.

The kitchen was next door to the dining room. He had a hole drilled in the wall so cups of tea could be sent in to him. He never made one himself. I never saw him washing a dish in my life. I think he thought that after you ate your dinner someone pressed a switch and, hey presto, everything was ready for the next meal.

One time when my mother had a migraine and couldn't make a cup of tea for him he didn't even know where to find the kettle. When he finally found it he put it on. When it started to boil he said, 'It's making a noise. What do I do now?'

We called the gap in the wall The Hatch. It was two feet thick and two feet high with a door on each side. If I curled myself up I was able to fit inside it when I was small. I liked going into it during games of Hide-and-Seek. I also hid in the loft sometimes, or even in the crook of the tree in our back yard. Another place that was suggested was Aunt

Nellie's room behind the wallpaper. I never quite found out where that was.

Sometimes I used to hide in the rafters behind the windows as well. They used to shake if a wind was blowing. That alerted people to the fact that you might be in there. Another good place to hide was the loft or under a bed or in the crook of the sycamore tree if you had the time. The 'seekers' usually counted to twenty. They were supposed to cover their eyes as you ran off but sometimes they didn't.

If the Hatch was open and my father was working I used to watch him from it. He had a rolltop desk with a cover on it. I used to love rolling it up and down. There was stationery and staplers and pairs of scissors and headed notepaper and lots of other things in the cubicles.

He had a special knife to open envelopes. It was like a scalpel. There were also rubber bands there. I used to take them sometimes to make catapults. He also had cards with his name on them that he gave to people. They said, 'Hugh Dillon-Malone, solicitor.' His address was at the bottom. He crossed out Bridge Street and put in Arthur Street instead. He was still refusing to call it Teeling Street.

There was a safe in the room as well, a huge green one. It weighed a ton. He kept most of his important documents there. There was a steel handle on it to open it. One day I took the key and buried it in the back yard. I don't know why. He was on the point of having a breakdown when he discovered it was missing.

Nobody was allowed leave the house until it was found. Every nook and cranny was searched, including the proverbial 'Nellie's room behind the wallpaper.' Eventually I said, 'I know where it is.' I led the family out to the yard like the Pied Piper and pointed to the hole. There were celebrations all round. My father was high with relief. I think he even lit a cigar. These were usually only brought out on special occasions.

When he was in good form there was no better company. He'd say crazy things like: 'Ha ha,' the man exclaimed in Portuguese.' He'd make mildly naughty quips: 'She opened the door with a sigh, and her pants became shorter and shorter.' Or he'd say, 'The way to spell 'bathing is 'pbathing.' The 'p' is silent.' He had a joke about a big-bosomed girl with a lisp who went to her doctor. 'Two big breaths,' the doctor said, 'Yeth,' she replied, 'and I'm only thiktheen.'

He'd talk about people's figaries: 'If you want to get someone to use their hands,' he'd say, 'Ask them what a spiral staircase is. Nobody has ever been born that can do it without gesturing.'

He played silly games with us. He'd put his hand under his chin and his tongue would come out. When he pulled his ear it would go in again. Another game he played involved him putting a sheet over his head and a torch under his chin. He'd turn the lights off and act like a ghost or a banshee. That scared the daylights out of us.

Other times he'd perform recitations, often closing his eyes to get himself into their world. It was the world of Lasca, trampled in a stampede in Texas, and Babette, a fallen woman. I often thought he lived in these worlds more than the actual one. He reminded me of what someone said of the 18th century actor David Garrick once, 'He was only acting when he *wasn't* on stage.' Why were such tragic figures so attractive to him? Was it because he believed, like the title of the essay he composed for me all those years ago, that our sweetest songs were those that told of saddest thought?

His favourite one was 'The Green Eye of the Little Yellow God.' He did it so much we almost knew it by heart. We'd be able to say the words with him but we couldn't match his emotion. He also did other recitations like

'Dangerous Dan McGrew and Omar Khayaam's 'If;' the two that everyone knew, as he put it.

'Lasca' was my favourite. Sometimes I thought he was imagining my mother as her. A lot of the lines seemed to apply to her like: 'Little knew she of books or creeds/An Ave Maria sufficed her needs.'

Another line went, 'She took the bitter and gave me the sweet.' She was like that with all of us. I don't think I ever remember her sitting down to a meal. She fed herself on scraps, like a bird.

Other parts of Lasca's character were nothing at all like my mother, like her possessive attitude towards the narrator. I always remember the lines:

'Once when I made her jealous for fun
At something I'd whispered, or looked, or done
She pulled from her garter a dear little dagger
And quick she plunged.
It made me stagger.
An inch to the left
Or an inch to the right
and I wouldn't be maundering here tonight.'

I loved the way he dramatized this vignette, and how he introduced me to strange words like 'maundering.'

Lasca dies at the end of the recitation. His eyes used to well up as he brought his alchemy to the words: 'And when I could rise, Lasca was…dead.' He always paused before the last word to give it the full emphasis. You'd see a tear in his eye. He'd be as sad as when Aunt Mary died. In the final verse he says, 'Sometimes I wonder why I do not care/ for the things that are like the things that were.' When you listened to him saying these words you felt he was talking about himself. If he was ever accused of living in the past he'd say, 'Why shouldn't I? It's better than the present.' There was no answer to that.

If he wasn't in good form he'd deliver the recitations in a workmanlike manner. We'd praise him but he'd be aware of having fallen below his standard. 'I didn't do it right,' he'd say. Our praise was no good to him. It was like the times when he was in bad form and we'd tell him he was looking good. 'It's not how I look,' he'd say, 'It's how I feel.' If we told him he looked distinguished he'd say, 'You mean *ex*-tinguished.'

The happiest time of his life, I always thought, was in the early years of his marriage. I wasn't around to see these but I heard about them from the rest of the family. He had good times when I was growing up too but not as many. As the years gained on him, the magic of his past wore away.

In the late sixties he started to drink more. In the pubs the romantic in him was able to recreate the magic of Trinity, to make himself believe he was still there even if the stories were different now and the people he was telling them to were only shadows of past friends. Alcohol was capable of overcoming such details by its transformative powers. It could turn a sow's ear into a silk purse.

I don't think any of us realised the toll the office fire had on him. After it plundered the building he'd gone to every day since he left Dublin he lost the interest in doing himself up. What was the point?

He became more nervous working from Norfolk than Bridge Street. When Uncle Louis died he didn't go to England for the funeral. He had a fear of flying. The ferry would have been an option but he hadn't time for that as the funeral was the following day. He felt Louis' wife, Eileen, didn't want him there.

He always thought she delayed telling him about the funeral until it was too late for him to go to it. Eileen had never got on with him. She thought he was too impractical.

Aunt Florence thought that too. She used to give out about him to my mother anytime she was out with her in Dun Laoghaire. My mother never listened to her when she did that. They got on fine apart from that one subject. It was obviously going to be no contest as to where my mother's loyalties lay whenever it came up.

Aunt Florence was a kind woman but she clashed with my father. It was probably the same way Aunt Eileen and Aunt Nellie clashed with him. They were 'straight down the line' people but he wasn't. He didn't like falling out with people but as he said, 'If you get on with everyone you're probably a man of straw.'

He liked quoting a line from George Bernard Shaw about an acquaintance: 'He hadn't an enemy in the world but none of his friends liked him.'

The family at Clive's Ordination

Changes

Some nights I saw my father deep in thought. He'd never say what was bothering him. When he was like that he retreated to his books and his recitations, maybe seeing solutions to his problems in these other worlds. I wanted to lift his burden, to make the chalice pass from him. Unfortunately I knew him well enough to know that wasn't going to happen.

The cinema was another form of escapism, for us as well as him. People often wondered how the Malones were able to afford to go to the Estoria so often.

In some ways he wanted to keep us as children forever. Maybe his mother had done that a little with him. He could have seen us as mirror images of his young self, people he wanted to keep in the bubble of privilege he enjoyed at Trinity. But of course that wasn't possible. There were too many of us. If he'd only had a few children like Uncle Louis he'd probably have sent us to boarding school. The fact that he couldn't do that made him feel bad.

He came out of such episodes in his own time. The sun would come in through the curtains the next morning and it would be as if they never happened. He'd be on about some book he read or some article he wanted me to access about his past.

We use words like 'bi-polar' to describe such conditions today. I've never appreciated terms like that. If he was bi-polar, so is everyone on the planet. He had moods like we all do and he came out of them like we all do.

I saw him trembling sometimes as he tried to light a cigarette. A pained look would come into his eyes. Going to the pictures even became an ordeal for him sometimes. He'd feel as if he was going to throw himself off the balcony. When he was at Mass he sat at the back of the church in case he got a panic attack. During the sermon he'd go out to the sacristy for a cigarette. Was it claustrophobia or nerves? Were they the same thing? In later years I'd experience the same sense of entrapment in lifts and airplanes and think: Was it my father coming out in me?

My mother went up to Dr Igoe one day to ask him if he could prescribe something for him. He told her there was a new pill on the market called Valium. She'd never heard of it before. None of us had.

The first time she gave one to him it worked like a dream. Afterwards she popped them into his mouth like jellybeans. They were like wonder drugs to her. Nobody knew about their addictive powers then. It was a bit like the way people didn't know the damage cigarettes were doing to people. After a while he didn't get as much out of them as that first time.

She usually gave him one when he was going to court. I'm not sure that was a good idea. A certain amount of nerves is a good thing. Singers sometimes say that if they aren't nervous they don't give a good performance. I think that was the way with him.

The courthouse was less than 100 yards from the Estoria. Geraghty's bar was just as close in the other direction. In one of these places he worked. In the others he performed, or watched others performing. One was work, the other play. Maybe their effect on him was mixed. Maybe the Estoria was his training ground for where he earned his daily bread.

I had my own ports of call. One was the Savoy, which I saw as a kind of poor relation to the Estoria. The Hibs was another and Muredach's a third. In these places I honed my other self in second homes, but I always went back to my first one to lick my wounds or recharge my batteries for an assault on life.

My father had already honed that life. As the sixties went on he seemed to be doing little but going through the motions of it, playing from a recycled script. In that sense he was doing little more than relaying lines like the Estoria actors, becoming a real-life Edward G. Robinson as he cross-examined guards in the witness box or pleaded with a judge to go easy on first time offenders.

I watched him in the same way I watched 'Ironside' or any of the other attorneys from the contrived programmes RTE bought from America, even then aware of the difference between packaged entertainment and the more convoluted scenarios teasing themselves out in front of my father in that dusty building on the Station Road.

His foot would be going ninety to the dozen the way it did when he was nervous as he waited for his chance to pounce on some legal point, the words already forming on his lips even before he spoke. He'd come in with, 'If I may, Judge,' or some such phrase, obeying all the decorum before landing a killer blow to the prosecution.

When I watched 'Columbo' in later years he reminded me of him. My mother liked Columbo even though he looked as if he slept in his coat. My father didn't, maybe for that reason, but he had the same technique of lulling witnesses into a false sense of security before pulling the ground from under them. It's interesting that Peter Falk, the actor who played columbo, called his autobiography, 'Just One More Thing.'

I was never in any doubt that it was his theatre. He needed the adrenalin. I often thought he'd have been more suited to being a barrister than a solicitor. He'd usually look tense heading off to it, walking up past the Estoria and the font with the crazy paving. He put on a show of being calm but he wasn't. My mother knew that, right from their first date on the boat.

When he didn't have court cases to contest he got more in on himself. He found it boring being in the house all the time. Drink became a temptation, a womb like Trinity, a ticket to the past.

When he was in hotels he drank mainly with other solicitors. In the bars he met the 'ordinary' people. He was more himself with them just as I was more myself with the people in the Hibs. His class consciousness went out the window at such times.

He always denied being a snob. 'Snobs pretend to be something they're not,' he'd say. Afterwards he'd go into the old rigmarole about his father, about his 'right' to have a double-barrelled name because of my grandfather's three marriages. I never liked him being defensive like that. As he said himself, when you're explaining you're losing.

He hated people who were trying to climb the social ladder. They were Johnny-Come-Latelys. My mother, on the contrary, was 'landed gentry.' How he loved using that phrase. And yet I never felt he looked comfortable when he was with the 'horsey' set.

One day he told me about a man he knew who was called Smith but who spelled his name as 'Smythe' 'He passes himself off as blue blood,' he said, 'but he's really only a five-eighth.'

I never knew what he meant by a five-eighth. He used the expression a lot. I think it was something to do with a tall hat.

My mother dealt with his clients when he wasn't up to it. He used to say she could have been a solicitor if she put her mind to it. 'We'll have to change the name on the plaque outside the door,' he said to her.

She had an easy manner with people. We used to say she could entertain a hobo in the kitchen and a bishop in the living room. He may have been the head of the house, as the saying went, but she was the neck, and it was the neck that turned the head.

She never gave out to him if he drank too much or if he was depressed. There was a line from the film 'The Alamo' that she liked quoting, 'You can't help being you, Travis, and I can't help being me.' She had the same attitude to any problems the rest of us gave her, having the knack of being able to split herself in nine different directions to deal with us.

Everything went back to normal when he was well. He saw the clients again and she went into the background.

If he was in especially good form he came to Enniscrone with us. My mother usually stayed in the house on such days. He'd order his hackney and we'd all pile into it.

Most of the time we cycled to Enniscrone instead of being driven. There were two roads to it, the Main Road and the Quay one. Some of us would take one and some the other. We'd have a race to see who got there first. Deezer always wanted to come with us. I had to lock him in the house to stop him following us. His tail would be wagging a hundred miles an hour with excitement. It made me feel mean but it was too dangerous to bring him.

If my father was with us we went in the taxi. I loved the smell of the leather. If it got too strong I rolled the window down and put my head into the wind. My heart used to leap when I saw the steeple of the Mexican church from Skermore Abbey, the roofless building where the two roads met.

He'd buy cones for us in the shop at the bottom of the hill beside the beach. If the day was hot, the ice cream would slide down the side of the wafer. You'd have to lick it sooner than you wanted to for fear of it falling on the sand. I bit the bottom of the wafer off sometimes and sucked the ice cream down through it. If you did that it went whoosh down your throat in a lump. You wouldn't be able to breathe for a few seconds.

If we were on our own we usually went to a place called the Valley of Diamonds. It was a dip in the dunes on the way to Bartra Island. He wouldn't have been able to walk that far, or to climb up to the top of the valley even if he was at it.

There were lots of seashells in it. When the sun was shining it made them sparkle like jewels. That's why we called it that. We used to dive down the hill on our stomachs as if we were on sleighs. When we got to the bottom we'd walk up to the top and then dive down again.

Sometimes we did that on the Convent Hill. There was ice on it in the winter. The hill curved at Arthur Wills' house where we got our milk. We used to slide around it. My father didn't like us doing that. You could slip onto the road and be knocked down if a car was coming.

One day in 1967 I tripped when I was climbing over a dune in Enniscrone. I hit my knee off a stone and it swelled up like a balloon. I was taken to Castlebar hospital to have it looked at. A doctor was going to lance it but in the end he decided to let the swelling go down naturally.

It was my Inter Cert year. I thought I was going to get off doing it but that didn't happen. I had to study Caesar and Livy and Virgil and Cicero from my hospital bed. As if being laid up wasn't bad enough.

'Hello, ducks,' the nurse who was treating me used to say to me when she came into the ward every morning. I was studying so much Latin I thought she meant 'dux,' like a leader.

The swelling went down eventually. I got out of hospital just before the 'Inter.' I thought I was going to fail it. My father told me not to worry if I did. He said he spent half his life failing exams. As if I needed to be told.

One night when I was cramming he told me to leave the books down and go to the pictures. 'Deathbed repentances never work,' he said. I took his advice, losing myself in 'The Dirty Dozen' in the Estoria on yet another one of Paddy Mulligan's free passes.

I squeezed through the exam by the skin of my teeth. When I showed him my results he gave me a fiver as a reward. 'It would have been double that if you failed,' he said, 'You've broken a family tradition.'

Mike Nichols' film 'The Graduate' came to the Estoria that year. I was too young to be allowed into it. I knew it was about a man who was dating a mother and daughter at the same time. We used to listen to the songs from it sung by Simon and Garfunkel.

My mother and father went to see it. She enjoyed it but he didn't. In some ways she was more liberal than he was. I remember her telling me how amused she was watching Dustin Hoffman trying to book into a hotel pretending he was on his own instead of with Anne Bancroft.

She liked other stars as well. Steve McQueen was her favourite. Maybe he brought out the mother in her. He had that 'little boy lost' look.

My father had no truck with any of these people. He wanted to be back in the world of the thirties gangster films, the world of James Cagney and Edward G. Robinson, Ramon Novarro and Ivor Novello. His embrace of the past was almost like a decision. He wouldn't let himself enjoy contemporary things. They represented a world he didn't want anything to do with.

He told me stories from the past, mystery stories and ghost stories written by people like Edgar Allan Poe and Somerset Maugham.

When he told them he became the people in them just like he became the people in the recitations he did. It was never a case of him acting a part. He got lost in them and because he did I did too, just as I got lost in his funny stories.

When he was funny he was funnier than everyone else and when he was sad he was sadder than anyone else. His highs were higher than most people and his lows were lower.

My mother saw more of his lows than the rest of us. She protected us from them and he did as well. He never wanted not to be happy, for our sake as much as his. The lows were like unwanted visitors inside his head that he did his best to get rid of.

Decision

As the sixties drew to a close, my father said he wanted to leave Ballina. When I asked him why he said, 'There comes a tide in the affairs of men. I've burned my boats.'

There were debts piling up and he was losing interest in his work. He talked about buying a house in Dublin, about everyone being in it together. It would mean a saving of rent for the members of the family that were already up there.

I asked him if he'd miss his friends. He said he didn't have any of those, only 'acquaintances.' Most of his so-called friends were 'boozing' pals rather than bosom ones. 'If we seemed close,' he said, 'It was the drink talking. We've all heard one another's stories *ad infinitem*. We're like bad actors in a play.' Would he miss them at all? 'If I never saw them again it'd be too soon.'

I told him I was sad to hear him dismissing a whole phase of his life. He said, 'Don't be. We drank together because we liked the drink more than each other. It was the glue that held us together.' He told me one of his friends drank so much he was put on a medication called Antabuse. It made you sick if you took alcohol with it. 'He almost died,' he said, 'That was enough for him. He felt drink was safer so he went back on it.'

Alcohol, my father always believed, brought out people's hypocrisy. 'They told me I was the bee's knees at bar counters,' he said, 'but behind my back they sniped. It got so bad I was afraid to go to the toilet. I was afraid my character would be taken in my absence. That's the thing about Irish people. They don't tell you what they think of you to your face. Maybe it comes from having been ruled by another country. We talk out of two sides of our mouth.'

I said I saw him having fun with people. 'The loud laugh,' he said, 'speaks the vacant mind.' Half the time, he said, he said he didn't know if they were laughing with him or at him. There was always that tension in him, wondering if people were genuine or not.

He had a thing about people wanting to pull him down. It went back to his father, his pedigree, the penny looking down on the ha'penny. That was why he told me never to explain how we got our double-barrel name. It was like a statement the actor Gregory Peck once made, 'If you have to tell people you're famous, you're not.'

'Most people are unhappy with their lives,' my father said, 'If you're doing better than them they want to bring you down to where they are. You become a target.'

He said some of his so-called friends plied him with alcohol to make him lower his defences, using flattery to make him open up about things he'd prefer not to have talked about. 'They palavered me to get me to say more than I wanted to,' was the way he put it.

He said he wanted to retire. 'All I want is a room somewhere,' he said. That and £6000.

It was always the same figure every time he brought the subject up. 'Why £6000?' I'd say. He had no explanation. Like the money he gave to Jimmy Geraghty each month for our groceries, it was a figure he plucked out of the air.

In the end he got his wish to leave Ballina. Plans were put in place to sell Norfolk. Paddy Murphy was going to buy it from us. He said he'd buy a house in Dublin that we could live in instead.

I didn't want to leave the town. It was as if the ground was being pulled from under my feet. I still had a year left in Muredach's. My father told me I wouldn't be able to finish that now.

Muredach's was never going to be my favourite place but I was more settled in it now than I had been in my first few years there. A priest had recently come to the college who said he didn't believe in striking children. He was progressive, bringing us out of the classroom to play games in the fields. He even organised table tennis tournaments for us in the Town Hall. I won one of them. It was probably because of all the practice got in Norfolk.

'What if I boarded there?' I said.

The words seemed to be coming from someone else's mouth rather than my own. Up until now I wouldn't have entertained such a prospect in a million years.

He said, 'Where would the money come from? And you're not cut out for boarding. You're even less cut out for it than me.'

I couldn't come up with a solution to the problem. No matter what way I thought, there was always an obstacle somewhere. Why was it that your circumstances always changed just when you didn't want them to?

One night shortly before we were due to leave, my mother told me she had breast cancer. I couldn't believe what I was hearing. She'd never said anything about it up to this. I heard her on the phone to Dr Igoe sometimes but I didn't know what it was about. One night when she was in bed I saw her sweating so much I got a fright.

'You need to be in hospital,' I said. She just laughed.

'I don't know what you're talking about,' she said.

She played it down just like she played everything down about herself. I never heard her talking about her miscarriages, her stillborn children, the twins Raymond and Mary who only lived a week. Why would she start now?

She said they caught it in time, that they were going to do a mastectomy.

'I'll be fine,' she said. If she was hanging off a cliff she would have said she'd be fine.

She was going to have the operation in Dublin. It made sense. We were going up there anyway. The facilities would be better. She'd have a more secure operation and better aftercare.

That news finalised things for me. I stopped asking to be left in Ballina. It was selfish of me to even think about it now. The move wasn't just about me. I had to realise that. It was about everyone. I was just a link in the chain.

Audrey and Jacinta were taken out of the convent now. Jacinta continued her studies in Dublin in the Loreto convent. Audrey decided to become a nurse. She was going to be doing her training in Surrey. My father was inconsolable at her leaving. He burst into tears.

He didn't cry often and he didn't like it when women did, describing tears as 'a woman's rhetoric.' But that day was different. He couldn't say, 'Mind yourself, pet' enough times to Audrey. As she disappeared down the runway at Dublin Airport, a man standing beside him didn't know what to make of it all.

'Where is she off to?' he said.

'England,' my father said, 'She's going to be a nurse over there.'

The man guffawed.

'The way you were crying,' he said, 'I thought she was on her way to a nunnery.'

1969

Everything happened fast in the summer of 1969. The house was sold. Furniture was stacked all over the place. People moved out. Sean MacDonnell started getting everything ready for the new owners.

It was the end of a decade and the end of my life as I knew it. I was the last person to leave Ballina. Audrey and Jacinta had left a few months earlier. My mother and father were also gone by now. My mother had to be in Dublin for her operation.

The cancer diagnosis meant she had to go off cigarettes forever. I knew how hard that must have been for her.

'How will you do it?' I said to her one night on the phone. It was a stupid question. How had she ever done anything difficult in her life? Without fuss.

'I'll find something else,' she said. It sounded like time to stock up on the Fox's mints.

I stayed on in Norfolk with Sean. He pulled the house asunder. I was disappointed to see him taking the banister off the stairs. I used to slide down it when I was young, taking care to stop before I hit the curl at the end.

Floorboards were even lifted up. Sean said he was going to re-wire everything. He knew a bit about electricity from his father. Tom MacDonnell had a shop selling electrical equipment on Garden Street as well as being an auctioneer.

I helped him as much as I could. We stepped over the floorboards to make cups of tea.

It was strange being with him on my own. Keith used to say there was always one spoon left in the wash basin when he did the dishes. I felt like that now, the last of the Mohicans. In a strange way I was glad it was just the two of us. I'd never had such independence before.

It was strange going down the town knowing that when I got back there'd be nobody in the house but Sean. Ever since I was a child there'd always be someone there, my father or mother or Tina or one of the family.

I thought I might feel lonely but I didn't. It was liberating knowing I could stay out as long as I liked and nobody would ask me where I'd been. I could go to the pictures or play snooker or walk down by the Moy and watch the fishermen taking in their catches.

One night I went down to the college and looked in the windows. It held no terror for me now that I was gone from it. The teachers could say what they liked and I didn't need to listen. They had no hold over me anymore, no way to influence what I did or didn't do.

When I got back to Norfolk I walked in and out through the empty rooms. Then I went out onto the roof that led to Gildy Ahern's orchard. The big field that you got to through a hole in the wall was at the other side of it. I sat there for ages looking at it. There was nobody to call me in for my tea, nobody to call me in for anything.

I knew I'd only have this freedom for a short time. The next time I came down to the house, whenever that was, there'd be other people there and it would be up to them whether they let me in or not. Maybe I wouldn't want to go in for fear of it bringing up memories, or maybe those memories wouldn't be there anymore because of all the changes Sean was making to the house before getting it ready to sell.

Some nights we sat sipping tea in the empty rooms. He told me about himself, how he never knew what he wanted to do with his life. He'd been staying away from home since he was in his teens, trying his hand at this and that. He was a jack of all trades, he said, and a master of none.

He was grateful to my mother for letting him stay with us. 'She never made a compliment out of it,' he said. He told me one night that he saw her as being as much of a mother to him as his own one. She had that way about her with most people she met.

He held an auction of all our possessions in the Town Hall shortly before I was due to leave Ballina. I helped him down the road with them. It was only a few doors away. I thought of myself listening to its music all the nights I couldn't sleep when I was growing up. I thought of all the people who'd met their husbands and wives at dances there on these nights, and all the families they'd raised, many of who never left the town. Now it was serving a different purpose, a more threatening one.

Over the next few hours I watched items of furniture that defined my youth being sold to strangers. I tried not to be emotional as I watched my father's collection of paperbacks being flogged for, as he might have put it himself, a 'fleabite.' How many years had he spent collecting them? One day, I always thought, I'd get to read them. Now that was never going to happen.

He wouldn't have allowed all this to go on if he knew about it. My mother didn't tell him much about what Sean was doing. She knew it would upset him too much. Her attitude was, 'Out of sight, out of mind.' Once we were leaving Ballina, she thought, we had to leave everything it represented for us as well, including our memories of it. Memories were luxuries we couldn't afford. There was too much to be lost by them when we were in a situation we could do nothing about.

Her attitude transmitted itself to him. As he prepared himself to leave the town he seemed to discard everything about it in his mind. It was like sloughing off a suit of clothes, like when the office burned down and he lost the interest in dressing himself up in Norfolk. Now Norfolk itself was gone, and everything else that went with it, including all those musty paperbacks that I was saving up for my adulthood to read.

After I went home I looked at the empty cabinet where the books had been. Only one book was still there. Sean must have overlooked it. It was a tattered copy of 'W.H. Auden's Selected Poems.'

It was sitting under the cabinet on one of the legs. My father had been using it to prop it up.

It had escaped the auction. On that account it became precious to me. It was a kind of victory over what was happening. I looked at the faded orange of the cover, the dog-eared pages inside. They seemed to be pleading with me not to throw them out.

There was no danger of that. They were much more precious to me than any mint-new book I ever saw anywhere else in the years ahead. I kept the book but never read it. I don't know why. For some reason I wanted it to be untouchable.

Keith and Clive's graduation

Dublin

The moon landing took place that year. I watched it with Sean in a room without furniture. There was just a bockety old TV set precariously balanced on a coffee table in the kitchen.

A man was discovering a new world and I was about to lose an old one. I looked at the television moon and then went out onto the street and looked up at the real one. It was much nicer.

The desolation of the moon's surface on the television reminded me of my own plight. Neil Armstrong was making his giant leap for mankind while I was dreading my own small step towards a city 150 miles away.

'It's a waste of money,' Sean said, 'They could have cured world poverty with what it cost to have someone in a suit walking across a few rocks.'

I saw his point. I'd grown up with the idea that there was a man on the moon. The romance was all gone now, the man being an astronaut.

I took a last walk around Ballina before leaving. The sun lay like a giant egg on the horizon. I went down the Killala Road past the national school and Aunt Nellie's house. She was inside but I didn't call on her.

I went down to Belleek where we used to play soccer. Afterwards I crossed the Moy and walked down to Bunree. It had a look of faded splendour.

I came home by the courthouse. My father would never enter it again. He said he didn't mind. I wondered if he was only saying that.

When I got back to Norfolk I looked out the window of the boxroom like I used to do with Ann. The old school was gone now. Everything looked different.

'Sometimes you only see things when you're about to leave them,' Sean said to me before going to bed. He slept in his house in Garden Street that night. Before leaving Norfolk he wished me well in Dublin. He said he'd be seeing me in a few weeks after chatting with Paddy Murphy about our transition.

I travelled to Dublin the following day in a car Paddy organised. It was a Station Wagon. There were three other people in it, all of them unknown to me. One of them had just come through a cancer operation. She was quiet. I felt sorry for her. She was very thin with horn-rimmed spectacles.

The other two kept asking me questions but I didn't feel like talking. I just watched the trees whizzing by on the side of the road. We had to stop at a road block at one stage. I said to the driver, 'I wish you could turn the car around and bring us back to Ballina.' He said, 'There's nothing there for you now, no house or no family.' I knew he was right but I didn't want to hear it.

As we drove through the various towns I thought of all the things I was leaving - the Estoria and the Savoy, the games of snooker, the trips to Enniscrone, the new term that would be beginning in Muredach's. I hadn't even said goodbye to my classmates.

As we got close to Dublin I found myself resenting my father. Why hadn't he worked for some more years? He could have done part time commissions until I saw my last year out at Muredach's.

I deserved to be allowed finish my education in a college I'd been in for four years. If I had, I might have considered staying in the town and maybe even practising Law there. Did he not consider the fact that I might one day want to do that?

He'd always warned each of us away from following him into the legal world. He joked that he'd disown any of us who became solicitors. Maybe everyone feels that way about what they do because they're doing it. It isn't an objective appraisal. When you're in any job you probably see the worst of it. Distance lends enchantment to the eye.

He once told me about a firm of solicitors in Sligo called Dooey, Cheatem and Howe. I believed him. In later years he enjoyed telling the joke about the gates of heaven being stolen by the devil. St. Peter wanted to sue him but he couldn't: All the lawyers were in hell.

He loved jokes about the hereafter. Another one he used to tell was about a man who presented himself at the pearly gates asking to get in. St. Peter asked him what good deeds he'd done in life. He said, 'I gave five bob to a tinker once.' St. Peter went to consult with God. He came back a minute later. The man said, 'Am I getting in?' St. Peter said, 'No. God said to give you your five bob and send you down to hell.'

The sun was going down as we got towards Dublin. I never saw so many houses in my life.

We reached O'Connell Street. Nelson's Pillar was gone from it. It made it look strange. In all the photographs I'd seen of it over the years and in all the postcards it was there, as much a fixture of it as the clock over Clery's.

It had been blown up in 1966, the fiftieth anniversary of 1916. I climbed it once when I was in the city on a holiday. I'd gone up to spend a week with our relations in Sandymount. I was glad to see it gone. Why should we have a British colonist on the main street of our capital city fifty years after achieving independence?

Hugo said to me one day, 'What's the difference between Napoleon and Nelson?' I said I didn't know. He said, 'One of them was Bonaparte and the other was blown apart.'

I looked at the cinemas around me. There were at least three of them. I thought we were doing well with two in Ballina. The driver of the car told me there were about a dozen of them altogether in Dublin. I was looking forward to checking them out, even without Paddy Mulligan's free passes.

We drove to 66 Cabra Park. That was where Keith was staying with Ruth. Clive was there as well. He was on a trip home from Africa.

I said goodbye to the people in the Station Wagon and walked towards the door. I stood in front of it for a few seconds before I knocked. Once I go inside, I thought, I'm crossing the Rubicon, as my father would have put it.

I rang the bell. Keith came out. 'Welcome to the big smoke,' he said. Ruth was behind him hoovering the floor. Gene Pitney was singing 'Looking Through the Eyes of Love' in the background. 'I hope you're not doing the place up for me,' I said. The two of them hugged me and brought me in.

'How are you feeling?' Ruth said after we were all sitting down. I said my head was buzzing from everything that was happening. She said not to be too lonely about Ballina. I said I'd try. She said my mother was going to have her operation soon. My father was in another hospital having different kinds of tests.

I told Keith I'd seen lots of cinemas in O'Connell Street. He said he'd bring me to any film I wanted to see. In a few days he was going to book seats for a new cowboy one that had just come out called, 'Butch Cassidy and the Sundance Kid.'

He loved cowboy films. 'Shane' was his all-time favourite. Everyone in the family saw it loads of times in Ballina. No more than my father's 'Green Eye of the Little Yellow God,' we practically knew the dialogue off by heart: 'I've come to get your offer, Ryker.' 'I'm not dealing with you, Shane.' 'You're dealing with me.'

They asked me about the auction. Ruth said all our lives were going to be different from now on. We were going to be moving from Cabra Park to another flat before going into the house Paddy Murphy organised for us. All the talk started to drain me. I asked them would they mind if I turned in early.

I spent most of that night tossing and turning in my bed. There was no music from the Town Hall to lull me to sleep. I thought of Paul Anka and Fabian and Adam Faith and Petula Clark and Brenda Lee and Buddy Holly and Billy Fury and all the others who sent shivers up my spine with their torch songs right through my youth.

Where were they now? Where was Jack Ruane and all the other bands who covered their songs when we had no Radio Luxembourg to transmit them to us? All I heard instead were dogs growling through the night, the sound of a distant train somewhere sending someone else somewhere they probably didn't want to go.

I wanted to go down to Syrons for chips. I wanted to have my bicycle fixed in Tommy Wards. I wanted to go up to O'Hora's for some sweets and broken biscuits to bring in to the Estoria with me. Why did everything have to change in life?

If I was older, I thought, maybe I wouldn't have felt as bad. Being the last in the line meant I never left home before. I'd have been better off if I felt I'd had enough of the town and all it represented.

Emotions hurt us. The less you felt, the luckier you were. But there was no point in trying to will yourself to be somebody else. You could only be yourself. I tried to turn my mind off the past. Some things were still there. I had to try and see the glass half full.

When I woke up the next morning I didn't know where I was for a few seconds. When I looked out the window I expected to see the old school and the Estoria but all I saw was a warren of houses circling around our little one. It made me feel like a prisoner. Was this the way things were always going to be?

Over the next few days I tried to accept my new situation. My father came out of hospital on the Sunday. He was a bit pale. It was strange being with him in a different house. I never had that experience before. We both felt like fish out of water. He said he was missing my mother. I told him I was missing her too.

I told him I was lonely for Ballina as well. 'Already?' he said. 'Maybe it won't be so bad after a while,' I said. He said, 'We can always go back for visits.' I wasn't sure I wanted to. Maybe it would only make me feel worse.

The following day he asked me to go into the 'Irish Times' office to get him a back issue of the paper that he missed. He had to have it every day for some reason. I went into D'Olier Street and asked for it at the desk. As I waited for the girl to get it I leafed through the pages of that day's edition. There was a review of 'Butch Cassidy' in it. It was headed, 'Bonnie and Clyde Go West.' Why did film reviewers have to try to be so clever, I thought. Could they not view a film on its own merits without comparing it to something else?

I sat around the flat in Cabra Park wondering where things were going to go from here. My father looked lost. Keith and Ruth did their best to spoil him when they were there but that wasn't all the time. They had jobs to go to and lives to live.

He missed the fact that he couldn't go walking round Ballina if he wanted. The fact that he rarely wanted to when he was there was beside the point. .

My mother came out of hospital. She looked well but surgery was surgery. It had to have taken its toll on her. Whenever we asked her about herself she changed the subject. What else was new?

Clive got me into a posh school called Belvedere. It was where James Joyce had gone. That meant nothing to me. I knew I'd be out of my depth there. I'd be with the sons of

Basil's graduation

people from the leafy suburbs of Dublin 4, people I'd have nothing in common with.

I'd have preferred to go somewhere like the O'Connell School in Richmond Street but I knew that wouldn't have 'done' for my father. He had too many grandiose notions to entertain the idea. He'd have seen it as the haven of those who were Non-U.

I never wanted to belong to a family that played croquet on the lawn and adjourned to the Blue Room for cucumber sandwiches. I'd have been bored to tears by a champagne and caviar lifestyle. If he thought he'd let me down by not offering me those things he didn't know me.

Uncle Louis might have wanted them. Paddy Dillon-Malone might have wanted them too, if not Stephen. All I wanted was to be able to get from one day to the next. I had no envy seeing Paddy Murphy drive around Ballina in a swanky car. If I was sent to Stoneyhurst I'd have spontaneously combusted.

The next few weeks are scrambled in my mind. The house Paddy organised for us turned out to be in a place called Iona Villas. It wasn't ready to move into yet. Sean MacDonnell was working on it. He'd arrived in Dublin shortly after me. As we waited for it to be ready we moved into a house not too far from the Cabra Park one in Phibsboro. It was in Shandon Drive. That meant I was going to be in four different houses in the space of a few months after spending sixteen years in just one. It was too much to take in.

Going into Belvedere was like submerging myself in treacle. Whatever misgivings I had about Muredach's, at least it had greenery around it. All Belvedere had was concrete. It was in the middle of a street. That meant it suffocated me in more ways than one. Smoke belched out of the surrounding chimneys.

I was put into a class called Rhetoric A. Even the name making me feel like someone in a St. Trinian's novel. Did they think I was clever? I didn't feel I was. A lot of the things we studied in Muredach's hadn't been covered in Belvedere. That made me even more confused than I already was. I kept my head down in class and watched the clock ticking interminably towards home time.

I tried to rid myself of the past like an old coat that didn't fit. The problem was that the new one didn't fit either. I malingered in the middle ground between a world that was gone and one that hadn't begun yet. I felt in freefall, daydreaming through the hours as teachers flicked their fingers in front of me to bring me back to a world of theorums, irregular verbs and battles fought more years ago than I cared to remember.

One day one of the boys in the class said to me, 'I don't know how you stuck life in a small town with everyone knowing your business. It would have crippled me.' I told him it didn't feel like that, that it wasn't people being curious, it was just human interest. 'You have hundred more places to go in the city,' he said. I said I didn't care about things like that. 'You're weird,' he said.

I thought he was the one who was weird. I felt I could see the world from my doorstep in Ballina. Maybe there were more varieties of people in Arthur Street than the whole of Dublin. Boring places created boring people. How could anyone interesting live in a skyscraper?

Having the family around me in the evenings was a bonus but it didn't mean as much to me as it would have in Ballina. The fact that they had to get up for jobs meant there were less late nights than there were in Ballina.

It felt strange waking up in a different building. One day after school I walked home to Cabra Park instead of Shandon Drive. A woman in curlers answered the door. She said, 'Who are you?' I replied, 'Who are you?'

Sean eventually told us we could move into the Villas. I was glad to be going into an actual house instead of rented accommodation.

It was situated off the Iona Road in Glasnevin, a red-bricked semi-detached house on a hill in a winding cul-de-sac. There was a small garden in the front and another one at the back with a garage at the end of it. Across the road there was a shop called, without too much imagination, The Hillside.

My father was full of questions. Where were we? Who were the neighbours? What kind of size was it? My mother told him we'd have to accept it even if we didn't like everything about it.

He went in. The kitchen was a long galley room. He thought it was tiny. After Norfolk's one it probably looked that way.

'You couldn't swing a cat in here,' he said.

'You said all you wanted was a room,' my mother said, 'not the Ritz.'

Life was different when you were confronted with something. He'd wanted to get out of Ballina so badly he thought anywhere would satisfy him. Now he reminded me of Norma Desmond, the character in Billy Wilder's film 'Sunset Boulevard.' She'd once been an icon and was now living in seclusion. Gloria Swanson's famous line in the film is, 'I didn't get small. The pictures got small.'

He shared her nostalgia for the glory days. He used to like singing the song, 'I dreamt that I dwelt in Marble Hall, with vassals and serfs by my side.' I told him he'd have to forget that nonsense now. We were doing well to have a roof over our heads and to all be together.

We called the house Norfolk just like the one in Ballina. Maybe we were trying to convince ourselves we could make it as much of a home as the Ballina one. Even though it was smaller than it, it had everything we needed.

The kitchen had an Aga cooker that took anthracite instead of coal. There was a glasshouse opposite it that caught the sun. There were three bedrooms upstairs. I was given a small one at the front of the house that had yellow wallpaper. I put a poster of Elvis on the wall.

On another wall I hung the cover of Bob Dylan's album 'Nashville Skyline.' It had a photo of him tipping his hat. I cut out the hat and suspended it from a string. When I pulled the string it made it look as if he was tipping his hat.

We were all like rabbits in the headlights for the next few days. Nobody talked much. We were all too busy trying to come to terms with our new surroundings. If there was anything we didn't like we were afraid to say it in case it set my father off.

At the end of the week I found a snooker hall nearby, the Cross Guns. If Iona Villas was going to be the new Norfolk, I thought, the Cross Guns could be the new Hibs. There was a tennis court nearby too. It was a place called Charleville on the Whitworth Road. Could that be the new Bunree? I was making desperate attempts in my head to try and convince myself that nothing had changed since leaving Ballina.

We developed routines as the weeks went on, doing our shopping in the Hillside as we once did in Geraghty's in Ballina. Every Tuesday a man drove a cart full of vegetables down through the Villas. He talked so much to my mother we used to joke that she was having a fling with him. My father had little cause to worry. He was hardly Tyrone Power in the looks department.

There was a dentist near the Cross Guns called Kevin O'Loughlin. Feena Murphy referred me to him. She was married to a dentist who knew him. She told me to visit him as soon as I was settled into the Villas.

He nearly had a seizure when he saw all my cavities. 'You have a sweet tooth,' he said. I told him all of them were sweet. 'If I did nothing for a month but eat sweets I wouldn't have as many as you,' he said. He arranged for a range of appointments for me.

He filled all my cavities over the next few months. I usually went into the Cross Guns for a game of snooker when I came out. My mouth would still be numb from the anaesthetic. It seemed to make me play better. I felt I had an unfair advantage over the other players because of it.

My father said he'd have preferred if he took all my teeth out instead of filling them. 'Dentists charge you a fortune for fillings,' he said, 'Then they extract them anyway when they can't make any more money out of them.'

He was as cynical about doctors as he was about dentists. Most of them were quacks as far as he was concerned. 'They're putting medicines of which they know little,' he'd say, 'into bodies of which they know less.' He liked telling a story about a doctor who had a son who entered the practice. After his first day seeing patients he went into his father. He said, 'I have good news for you. I cured Mrs McCarthy.' Mrs McCarthy was a hypochondriac. The father said, 'You fool. I left her to you as a legacy.'

He told me he knew a man who got a clean bill of health one day and then dropped dead the next.

'Whenever I go to a doctor I like him to find something wrong with me,' he said, 'something small preferably, to make the visit worthwhile.'

He liked telling a joke about two surgeons arguing about a patient they were operating on. One of them says to the other, 'I bet the autopsy will prove I'm right.' Another quip was, 'The operation was successful but the patient died.'

The reason doctors wore masks at operations, he claimed, was so they wouldn't be recognised when they made a mistake. The reason their writing was so bad was so you wouldn't know what they were charging you. We had a relative from Scotland called Brady. He used to say 'The best part of a hospital is the *ootside*.' My father empathised with that sentiment.

He had a friend in Ballina called Martin McGrath who had an ulcer. He had an operation but it didn't help so he went back to his surgeon. 'Come in next week and we'll have another peep,' the surgeon said. Martin shot back, 'The last 'peep' cost me £200.' He loved telling stories like that. They were simple but we still laughed. Maybe we laughed as much at him as at the stories. We'd heard most of them before.

He couldn't settle in Dublin. He was, as he put it, 'in it but not of it.' He made trips into the city centre every now and then but didn't enjoy them. I think he expected to be recognised wherever he went. It was strange for him walking down streets and knowing nobody.

'I used to be a big fish in a small pond,' he said, 'Now I'm a small fish in a big one.' It was like Norma Desmond after her film career capsized in 'Sunset Boulevard.' I said to him 'Why should you care about things like that? You're retired.' He said, 'I didn't think I would.'

I didn't settle in Dublin any more than he did. Even though there were fifty years between us we were strangely similar, two poles of the same uprooting.

Ballina kept coming into my mind. I saw it in every street, every building. He brooded about the past while I brooded about Ballina.

He was out of his time and I was out of my place. He dreamt he dwelt in Marble Hall and I dreamt I dwelt in Arthur Street. It was different being a son than a father. I had no responsibilities growing up. He had nine of them, ten if you count my mother. That's the difference between youth and age, between innocence and experience. As he might have said himself, 'Uneasy is the head that wears the crown.'

Basil went to America soon after I went to Belvedere. He had great success in business. I didn't think he'd have any trouble in that area because of his quick intelligence. He donated his Honda 50 to me. 'Bring it into the college with you,' he said. I told him I'd be too inhibited to do that. Some of the other pupils had motorbikes but I couldn't see myself being like them. In Muredach's most of us had crocks.

I tried to make the best of life in Belvedere. It was more civilised than Muredach's in the sense that we weren't beaten but it bored me to tears. 'Maybe you'd like it more if you played rugger,' my father said I couldn't resist replying, 'I hate the game as much as you did when you were my age.' A priest called Fr Moran tried to get me to play it. I told him it held no interest for me. There were too many stoppages in it.

'If it was a train going from A to B,' I said, 'the driver would be sacked.' He said my negative feelings were due to the fact that I hadn't played it in Ballina. He was probably right but that didn't change my attitude. We were all, as my father put it, 'vicissitudes of our environment.'

I had little in common with the other pupils. A lot of them knew one another almost from birth. I was a stranger to them so they didn't bother getting to know me. I could hardly blame them. At the end of the day they were jackeens and I was a culchie – or rather a dulchie. They had much more confidence in themselves than we had in Muredach's. It resulted in them giving lots of backchat to the teachers. You'd nearly have been expelled for that in Ballina.

One of the priests who taught us ran the Belvedere Newsboys Club. He was a lovely man but he couldn't keep control of us. Everyone made fun of him. Some of us

Aunt Valerie & Uncle Michael

used to jump up on the window sill to test him. He'd be going, 'What are you doing up there?' instead of ordering them to come down. Another priest, the one who taught us Latin, was obsessed with someone called Octavian that I'd never heard of before. He glided into the classroom every day like a ghost.

I told my mother I felt like a fish out of water. 'You'll be fine once you get into the swing of things,' she said.

I don't think I ever did. It's difficult going from a school where you know everybody to one where you know nobody. The teachers didn't hit me so at least that bad part of Muredach's was taken away but I didn't relate to the other people in my class. Every positive had a negative. God never opened one door but he closed another.

There were two cinemas near us, the State and the Bohemian. The State showed European films sometimes. The Bohemian was more low rent. We called it the fleapit. I doubted if either of them could come close to the Estoria or the Savoy for me. No matter how good the films that were showing, I had no sentimental connection to them.

Tina left us that year as well. She found it as hard to adjust to the change in her life too. I thought of her as being like me. She went to other houses but it wasn't the same. You can't be yourself in another environment no matter how many times you try and tell yourself you can.

I wondered if my father was going through the same thing. He was glad to be installed in a new place and to have my mother back from hospital. But nobody could just stop doing what they were doing for thirty years without feeling strange.

Retirement is different for everyone. Some people just want to prune their petunias. Others have a bucket list after spending forty years pushing a pen. They want to travel the world or write the Great Irish Novel or maybe a thesis on the mating habits of the duck-billed platypus. My father went into a room and more or less stayed there for the rest of his life, making brief sojourns out to the kitchen and briefer ones outdoors.

Every night he put the chain on the front door like he did in Ballina. It was yet another example of him keeping the world out as he retreated to the cocoon of his files, his newspapers and my mother. Sometimes he reminded me of a child as he lay asleep beside her, all the pain of Ballina burnt out of him even if he wasn't willing to admit it.

They say a man's house is his castle. The bedroom was his one. That was where he looked out at the world with his all-seeing eye, the green eye of the little yellow god, and pointed out what was wrong with it. He told us it was going to hell in every possible way – religiously, politically, intellectually. It was like a metaphorical version of the Titanic except for the fact that we weren't singing 'Nearer My God to Thee' as we went down.

Apart from the family he didn't really see anyone in Dublin. The family was his life but we had our own lives too. Some nights he'd get elated telling us things late at night and we'd be too tired to listen. He'd be getting warmed up for some story and suddenly someone would say they had to go to bed. It wasn't anyone's fault. We were just at different phases of our lives. We had places to go the next day and he didn't.

One night he was in the middle of telling me some story when my mother was in the kitchen. She was washing some socks in the sink at the time.

She turned round. He thought she was going to ask him something about his story but all she said was, 'Would either of you like a hot water bottle?'

She was so practical. It was like the way she often offered us food when we were in another world. She'd spot if you were hungry when you didn't even know you were yourself. Now she was sussing that we were probably cold.

My father looked at her as if he didn't know what she was talking about. His face fell. All I could do was laugh.

Somehow I got through the year. My ambition was to get a piece of paper called the Leaving Cert and I achieved that. I got four honours. It was a relief. They meant I qualified for university.

My father wanted me to go to Trinity but I knew I'd be as much out of my depth there as I was in Belvedere. I chose UCD instead, or 'National' as he called it.

I didn't know what I wanted to do there. It was always the way with me. I wasn't like Clive or Basil who had their eyes firmly fixed on futures that were going to fulfil them.

Clive said he knew he wanted to be a priest from the age of twelve. Keith was more worldly. I heard Clive discussing religion with my father sometimes. Keith was more likely to be talking to him about films or horses.

It was strange living with the family. When I was growing up I only saw my older brothers and sisters at holiday times. They'd arrive in a flurry of excitement at the train station and then before you knew it they'd be gone again.

When I was with them all the time I got to see their daily lives. They might be rushing for a bus or going to have a clothing item cleaned or be stressed over something that happened at work. It made them more real, just like it made my father more real to them to have him with them all the time.

Hugo left All Hallows that year. He was near ordination at the time so it was a big surprise. 'I can't breathe in there,' he said. He was with Keith and me when he told us he was leaving. We were playing a game of tennis at the time. Keith thought he was joking but I felt he wasn't.

He told everyone else later that evening. The house came to a standstill. My father was the most surprised of all. He'd seen Clive being so sure of his vocation.

Clive was free of the doubts of Jesuits like Gerard Manley Hopkins or even Teilhard de Chardin. Hugo grew up in a different world. He welcomed the winds of change blowing through the Vatican, the kind of change elucidated by Bob Dylan in his famous song. Nothing was sacred in the sixties, not even God.

Someone once said that having a priest in the family in Ireland in the fifties was like having a pop star in it for a later generation. That was the way things were in Ballina. We used to joke about streets having competitions with one another to see who could produce the most. Tommy Tiernan once said, 'We grew them like potatoes.'

My father had a large family connection to priests. He was proud when Clive and Hugo entered seminaries but would never have put pressure on either of them to do so. He realised how different they were in their vocations. His own theology was closer to Clive's.

Hugo embraced the changes that were coming about in the church in the late sixties. My father was upset by them. Clive's vocation was too strong to be bothered either way. The idea of him leaving the Jesuits because of the changes would have been as difficult to contemplate as the sun stopping itself shining.

Hugo was different. As the sixties exploded into our world he started 'finding himself,' as the expression went, when he entered All Hallows. That process took many twists and turns over the next decade as he became fascinated by everything from liberation theology to the revolution of Vatican II.

All Hallows fulfilled Hugo in a way Muredach's never could have but in the end it wasn't enough for him. He left it for what John McGahern once referred to as 'the lay priesthood of teaching.'

Clive inhabited both. Maybe he was lucky to have entered the Jesuits before Pope John 23rd became Pope. His decision was made long before the sixties played havoc with all the old verities. Hugo embraced the cultural shift that took place under Pope John with both hands. He now said he wanted to go to university.

'How are we going to afford that?' my father said.

'You were over a decade in Trinity,' Hugo pointed out.

'That was different,' my father said, 'We had the money.'

I thought of the man in 'The Graduate' advising Dustin Hoffman to go into 'plastics' because that was where the future was. Both Hugo and myself were like Hoffman's character, unsure of where our futures lay.

A few other seminarians Hugo was friendly with started to come round to the Villas now. The months fled by in a swirl of late nights and sing-songs. We sang oldies from 'Oklahoma' and 'Showboat' and some newer ones from people like Simon and Garfunkel. One of them, a man called Jim O'Mahony, expressed a romantic interest in June at one stage. I thought he might leave too but he stayed on, eventually becoming right hand man to a bishop in Hawaii.

Sometimes as I listened to the music I closed my eyes and imagined myself back in Ballina. It was like the way my father did when he was trying to make himself believe he was in the world of Babette, of Lasca, of the man from Kathmandu who got the Colonel's daughter to smile on him in 'The Green Eye of the Little Yellow God.' Then I'd open them again and I'd be back in boring Dublin.

Hugo and myself started in UCD together. He did Arts. I signed up for Commerce. Ireland had just gone into the EU, or the Common Market as it was then called.

Keith thought I'd get a good job out of the Commerce degree. He wasn't happy in his own one. Nobody was, he said. They just did them because they had to. He was working in a factory in Finglas called Unidare.

‘I have no interest in being promoted, he said, ‘My ambition is to stay where I am.’

I started going to another snooker hall now, one called the Cosmo in O’Connell Street. I’d been there once or twice before when I came to Dublin to stay with our relation Joan O’Reilly in Sandymount. It was a dingy place in a basement that you got into by banging on a steel door. All the ‘Hards’ hung out there, people on the fringes of crime who’d grown up on the wrong side of the tracks. There’d be vomit outside the door sometimes, or even blood, as it disgorged its night’s detritus. I watched people falling into cars as they left it, watched taxis slinking their way to the suburbs like giant beetles with them on board.

I often stumbled out of it in the middle of the night feeling I’d had some kind of baptism by fire into their ways. My father would usually be up when I got home.

‘You must really love your snooker,’ he’d say.

I’d tell him it wasn’t just the game, it was having somewhere to go where you could connect with people. The Cross Guns had become a bit too tame for me. There was an edge to the Cosmo that I imagined Alex Higgins found in the Jampot in Belfast or Jimmy White in Zan’s in East London, a feeling of electricity in the air as if you never knew what was going to happen from one moment to the next.

‘I suppose you meet all the down-and-outs there,’ my father said to me one night. I said I didn’t think of them like that. They were rough, I said, but mostly kind-hearted. ‘That’s all that matters,’ he said.

I told him I’d stop going there if he wanted but he said there was no need for that. He had no problem with it. He’d softened since the Ballina days when he’d warned me away from the Hibs. I didn’t know why. Maybe the fact of his being uprooted from his world made him lose his old attitudes.

The Cosmo, like the Hibs in my Ballina days, became a home from home for me in time. I felt sorry he had no places to go to himself. Dublin had been such a buzz for him when he was young. Now it was just, as he said, 'a room.' He was like the salmon swimming upstream to where he was spawned to live out his last years.

He didn't make any attempt to get to know the people around us, the Mackens to our left or the Caseys to our right. I only knew them slightly myself. Marius Casey became a friend of all of us, especially June.

Her father had angina. He was very systematic. My mother used to see him out mowing the lawn sometimes. She was fascinated by how fastidious he was about it.

'It's as if every blade has to be exactly the same size,' she said, 'If it isn't, he'd almost go into the house to get a pair of scissors to cut it.'

University

I droplanded into Commerce like the sheep I was. It was a yawn of a year. Every morning I got the 22A bus from Phibsboro to the campus in Belfield. I jotted down notes that I was expected to trot out the following summer in the examination hall in the RDS.

There were a lot of girls in the class. Chauvinist that I was, I didn't expect that. The cliché was that girls weren't good at Maths. Between lectures I saw them reading business journals.

It wasn't like being in university. It was more like an extension of Belvedere.

'You're living in the wrong time,' my father told me, 'People don't know how to have fun anymore.'

He was always waiting for me when I got home. He'd ask me how I'd got on, what people I met. It was as if his world was over and mine beginning.

I was sorry I didn't have interesting stories for him. He'd had so many for me over the years, ones I rarely listened to. Why didn't I? Maybe because the people he was telling me about were so far away in time.

Not having known any of my grandparents made his youth seem even farther away than it was. I tried to cobble a few stories together to entertain him but even as I was telling them to him I was aware of how trite they were.

'I have no social life in Belfield,' I told him, 'It's like secondary school all over again.'

He said, 'He travels fastest who travels alone.'

In time he grew to accept the fact that I was in 'National' instead of Trinity. He became more like the rest of the family in his behaviour. It was strange to see him watching the TV shows we all watched, shows like 'Kojak' with its 'Who loves you, baby?' tagline and 'Hawaii Five-O' with its 'Book him, Dano.'

He also got to like 'Coronation Street' but wouldn't admit it. It was 'infra dig.' He'd change the station if we came into the room. He also watched legal programmes like 'Perry Mason' and 'Arrest and Trial.' I bought into their falseness like most other people, eventually starting to think that they were more authentic than anything I witnessed in the Ballina courthouse. My father wasn't so easily fooled. He hated the way they misrepresented court cases with dramatic exposures in the final reel.

'That would never happen in the real world,' he'd say, 'Every lawyer knows what a case is about as soon as he starts it.'

I'd say, 'It's a film, not life,' but it wouldn't do any good. 'Why do they bother making these things if they don't want to get them right?' he'd say. He hadn't been as judgmental in the Estoria, maybe because escapism was allowable on the big screen. He wasn't on the balcony now but in the parterre, contenting himself with 'the box' because nothing else was available.

There was a show called 'Rowan and Martin's Laugh-In' that he hated with a vengeance. It had canned laughter in it. You saw the actors waiting for the laughter to die down before they said their next lines. It was as if they were hearing it themselves but you knew they weren't. It wasn't a live show. They were told by the director that it was going to be put in.

That's how false American shows were, and how false Ireland became once we started importing them instead of making our own ones. Being told when to laugh, and for how long, was anathema to everything about the spontaneity of my father's life, of his ability to entertain. It was the beginning of an epidemic of formula programmes RTE bought because they were cheap, the beginning of our culture being stolen by bland conglomerates.

Some nights I'd see him watching the television screen in a daze. It was as if he wasn't even seeing it. I'd wonder what thoughts were going through his head, what memories were intruding. Why did any of us have to get old, I'd think, why did the good times have to stop?

I tried to get him in on things I was interested in but it was a losing battle. He didn't like the films I went to or the music I listened to. Elvis Presley was a baboon in his view. Most other pop singers were little more than an assault on his eardrums.

He wrote letters to the 'Irish Times' inveighing against the way the world was going, about how people lied and cheated to get to the top, the increasing violence everywhere you looked. He also wrote to the paper about other issues like the acres of wheat that were burned every year in America to keep the prices high instead of giving them to the poorer countries. In some ways he was like a Victor Meldrew before his time, or the character in Greek mythology who tried to stop the tide.

He was almost undressed without the 'Times.' To his way of thinking it was the paper that was read by 'the best people.' The 'Irish Press' was 'infra dig.' Even the 'Irish Independent,' the so-called 'Blueshirt' paper, was.

He read books that were recommended by the 'Irish Times,' ones that were reviewed in its pages every Saturday. He trusted the writers of these reviews to guide him towards ones he'd enjoy. 'I want something with a beginning, a middle and an end,' he'd say.

My own tastes ran in a different direction. The books I recommended to him, he said sometimes, seemed to end in the middle. 'Modern writers aren't worth a curse,' he'd say, 'They're all codswallop.'

He read a history book I recommended to him that impressed me but it did nothing for him. It was full of waffle in his eyes, sensationalism for the sake of it. Why couldn't modern writers just call a spade a spade?

'All the great ones are dead,' he declared, 'like the great everything else's. The ones that were living were mostly 'humbug.' So many things he didn't like were 'humbug.' It was a great word of his.

He disparaged the cult of celebrity that was coming in. 'When everyone is someone,' he said, 'no one is anyone.' Artists were getting enormous sums of money for junk. He told me about a painting that was hung upside down in a gallery and nobody noticed.

I felt he'd enjoy the modern world more if he gave it a chance. It was as if he'd trapped himself into a dismissal of everything he saw around him. Once he'd created the image he had to live up to it.

He disparaged the phenomenon of the New Man. If he saw one wheeling a pram he thought of him as a sissy. 'They'll be having babies yet,' he'd say. He wasn't far wrong in that.

Feminism was anathema to him. 'A mannish woman,' he said, 'is the worst of men.' I wondered how he'd have been if he married a feminist. Was my grandmother one? My grandfather had to accept the fact that she wanted to keep her maiden name. He mightn't have wanted that. How would my father have been if my mother wanted us to grow up as Conry-Malones? How about if we were Conry-Dillon-Malones? It was bad enough growing up with two names. Having three would have done my head in.

One day he said to me, 'I think it's a crime to bring a child into the world.' I said, 'It's a bit late for you to be saying that.'

He got onto the subject of sex, something he didn't talk about much. Women, he said, were wearing skirts up to their bottoms to show off their legs. 'Vanity thy name is woman,' he'd say. He didn't mind them wearing them short but why did they keep pulling them down after they did that? 'They knew what length they were when they put them on,' he'd say, 'Be one thing or another.'

Most of the programmes he watched on television, he said, had 'smut' in them. 'Your mother and myself haven't bothered about any of that kind of thing for years,' he said. After thirteen pregnancies, I thought, I hoped so. He said he was bored by all the naked bodies on display in modern films. Far more erotic was something that 'hinted at what it hid.'

The only 'smutty' book I remembered him talking about in Ballina was 'Lady Chatterley's Lover.' There was a copy of it circulating with half the town's fingerprints on it. It seemed to represent some kind of victory for a person to thumb through its pages. You didn't have to read it. Far better was to chortle about it in pubs.

D.H. Lawrence was synonomous with eroticism at the time. I doubt if my father was aware of other erotic writers. If he was he would have had no time for them, 'good, bad or indifferent,' to use one of his favourite phrases.

I don't remember him ever talking about James Joyce's 'Ulysses.' Maybe that's because it wasn't banned. It was just sold under the counter. An Irish solution, as they said, to an Irish problem. So often we were neither one thing or another, our culture suspended on a tide of uncertainty, a nudge and a wink.

The attraction of Lawrence seemed to be like the attraction of after-hours drinking or any other kind of forbidden fruit for him. 'Nothing like the shutters coming down in Ballina,' he said, 'made solicitors more thirsty.'

My parents outside the Gresham Hotel

Adjustment

The months dragged on. I got the 22A bus into Belfield every day. The branches of the trees on the Stillorgan Road rattled the windows as we got close to the campus. I carried heavy tomes with me into the lecture halls. The lecturers talked about money as if it was a god. It had to be, I thought, if all the people listening to them, me included, were giving it so much attention. Did all accountancy students sell their souls like this over the centuries?

In between lectures I went to the cafeteria. Sometimes one of my classmates, Mick, came with me. One of the waitresses liked to go scantily clad. One day I said to Mick, 'That's some dress she's almost wearing.' He didn't register anything. Maybe he was more interested in other kinds of figures.

Leaves fell from the trees as October came in. I trudged through them with the rest of the students as we made our way to Theatre L. We filed in like robots, jotting down facts and figures as autumn turned into winter, the winter of our discontent. It was like eating porridge studying dull economists, duller mathematicians.

One night I showed my father one of the denser ones. After flipping through it he said, 'If you can understand this, you're a better man than I am, Gunga Din.' I said his law ones were probably even more complicated. 'I had ten years to digest them,' he said, 'You have only one.'

The only way I got through it was by reading my own kinds of books in the evenings. I felt the writers I liked were better than my father's ones. Why would I read Hilaire Belloc when I could have Norman Mailer? Why would I bother with Chesterton when I could have Gide? I did my best not to talk to him about subjects like that. They were only going to cause tension. Instead I picked more neutral topics.

He came to life when the subject of the family came up. One night in 1971 he recorded a speech on a cassette about all of us. Hugo sat at the end of his bed playing a Simon and Garfunkel song on his guitar called 'The Dangling Conversation.' He strummed the guitar as my father spoke. He went through all of us in his speech, the ones who were at home and the ones away.

Basil was in Oklahoma at the time. At one stage he considered staying there. He was adventurous. He'd have thought nothing of upping sticks if the opportunity for some new challenge was there.

Clive was still in Zambia. I thought of Basil being 3000 miles away and Clive maybe 5000. To my father both places were like the far side of the moon. 'The favourite in the family is the sick one,' he said in his speech, 'or the one farthest away. But paradoxically none of you is away because you're always on our minds.'

I wondered if Hugo picked 'The Dangling Conversation' because of my father being so sentimental. There was a line in it about people being 'like shells upon the shore' in their isolation. Was that how he felt about Clive and Basil being so far away?

He ended the tape with one of his trademark quips to Basil, 'God bless you, my son, as the atheist said.'

My mother was asleep beside him in the bed. In an afterthought he added, 'She wakes up now and again,' he said, 'wondering if she's having a bad dream.'

She went through terrible times every time someone left home. It was worst with Clive because he'd be gone for so long. She tried to busy herself around the kitchen to take her mind off him being gone.

It was something she had to work out of herself every time. She cried when he came home as well. That was okay because they were tears of joy. My father tried to keep a stiff upper lip at such times but he wasn't very successful at it, as he proved that day at Dublin Airport when Audrey was going to Surrey to train to be a nurse. I never found myself in the position of having to say goodbye to either of my parents for any long period as I only went out of Ireland for the summers. I may have had wanderlust but I was also a homing pigeon.

I continued to take the bus into Belfield every day, trying to make the best of a course that was draining the life out of me. In some ways it was like being back in Muredach's. One day I was talking to someone beside me during a lecture and the lecturer looked up at us. He said, 'Is someone talking up there?' I couldn't believe something like that could happen at third level.

Suddenly it was summer. We had our last lecture one sunny day. The year was ending like it did in Muredach's and Belvedere and everywhere else. Nothing had changed. I was off the hook for another twelve months.

I folded my jotter and went out to the lake. The sun gorged out like a ball in the sky, streaking the water before being swallowed up by it. I lit a cigarette like some form of exhumation. Had I learned anything? Did I care?

I regurgitated the data that was fed to me at the lectures in an examination hall in the RDS with my fellow robots, charting the demographics of debits and credits like Keith did a decade or so before me. Did I want to follow his footsteps into somewhere like Unidare? Would I have a choice? It wasn't the Roaring Twenties and I wasn't my father. Reality was biting. A desk awaited me in some microchip firm in two more years so I could sell my soul to it until retirement loomed. Or not.

I just about scraped through the exams at the end of the year. After they were over I went to London for the summer. The night before I got on the plane my father said to me, 'You're doing something I couldn't.' I thought about how he must have felt after Uncle Louis died. 'It isn't easy for me either,' I said. Even though it was only a short flight I was still concerned about claustrophobia on the plane.

A friend of Hugo's got me a job in a bar called The Blackstock in London. It was mainly patronised by Irishmen. The night I arrived, the head barman gave the manager two black eyes and then robbed the till before legging it out the door. It turned out he was a fugitive from an asylum in Scotland. I thought to myself: This is going to be an interesting job.

There were some English customers as well as Irish ones. They gave me flak about the IRA. The 'Troubles' had now extended to England. Some bombs were going off.

I found myself getting into arguments with them about what they'd done to our country for 700 years. I'd never said these sort of things to people in Ireland. We all become patriots when we leave home. 'Someone should take the North of Ireland,' the manager said to me one night, 'and drop it into the Atlantic.'

I wondered if Audrey and Jacinta got any abuse on account of being Irish. Jacinta had left the city by now. Audrey was down in Surrey so she was probably insulated from it. At the weekends I visited Aunt Valerie, my mother's sister. She'd been with her on her first date with my father all those years ago on the boat. Herself and her husband Michael were living in reduced circumstances on the outskirts of Stoke Newington.

They had money at the beginning of their marriage. Michael squandered it all gambling. He was said to have put £50,000 on a horse once. I shudder to think what that would be worth today. 'They were left without a brass farthing,' my father said. One generation made the money, it seemed, and the next one spent it.

I didn't blame Michael. He had an addiction. I tried to talk to him about it once or twice but it was obvious he didn't want to. He kept to himself most of the time I was there and I tried not to intrude on that.

Aunt Valerie was a lady. She never complained even though Michael had lost everything they had. Living on the breadline wasn't what she had in mind when she married him. She must have been thinking of a life in high society. They probably had that before his addiction kicked in. Now she was just another person in a house, a person people passed on the street without knowing where she'd come from, how far down the ladder she'd fallen from those halcyon years.

The first time I visited her I told her my boss in the pub was 'a fussy character.' I told her he made me wash glasses to within an inch of their lives. When I saw her the next week the first thing she asked me how was the 'character.' She'd never heard the word applied to a person instead of someone in a film. I was touched by the fact that she was interested in my little life when her own one was in such turmoil.

No matter how poor they were, Valerie and Michael felt like royalty to me. Michael wore his dressing gown most of the time. He reminded me of my father in that. Valerie was more like my mother, an aristocratic woman ministering to an eccentric husband. They should have been living in a mansion, I thought, instead of a council house in the middle of nowhere.

At the end of the summer I went to France with Hugo. We spent most of our time picking grapes. It was a weird time, getting up at the crack of dawn every day. We worked our backs off in the searing heat and then came home to a little cabin where a courtesy bottle of wine would be plonked on the table for us by the *patron*.

We called into the Blackstock on the way home. One night after closing time we had a few drinks. We started talking about Belfield.

Hugo told me he didn't think I was cut out for Accountancy. The more I listened to him, the more I realised he was right. I probably always knew it but I needed someone else to say it to me. On the spur of the moment I decided to scrap the Commerce degree and do one in Arts instead.

When I got back to Dublin I was wondering how I'd tell my father about my decision. He'd already had to deal with Hugo changing horses in mid-stream.

I knew how much he worried about money. The fees weren't too bad for me because of the fact that I'd got four Honours in the Leaving Cert. They qualified me for some kind of grant. It was a help but I wasn't in a job like the rest of the family so it probably didn't mean much.

I wondered if he'd be mad at me when I told him what I planned to do. He'd always been understanding to me as a child whenever I was in any sort of quandary. How would he be now that I was a so-called adult? I took a deep breath as I walked in the door.

My mother was the first person I saw. She fussed over me the way she always did, asking me all the questions mothers did, like whether I ate enough and kept myself warm. Then he appeared. He looked serious.

Before I got a chance to say anything he said, 'We had to put Deezer down.' I couldn't believe what I was hearing. The speech I'd prepared in my head went out the window.

'What are you talking about?' I said.

'He bit a girl under the eye,' he said. I couldn't believe that either.

'What are you saying?' I said. I was trying to take the words in, to link them together.

He told me to sit down. My mother went over to the kettle to make tea. My heart was beating fast as I sat down.

He said Deezer bit a girl under the eye. There were rumours about her parents taking an action against us. He'd had a similar case in Ballina some years before that involved a huge pay-out.

'So he's dead,' I said.

'I'm sorry,' he said.

I found myself getting annoyed with him. I'd never seen him playing with him. Did he dislike him? Was he waiting to get me out of the way for an opportunity to do something to him?

I started crying. He'd been my friend ever since we rescued him that day from his owner in Lord Edward Street. I played with him every day of my life. Sometimes I even talked to him as if he was a human being. Now I'd never see him again.

He wasn't an aggressive dog but sometimes I 'play-fought' with him. There was a mat at the bottom of the stairs in the Villas. I'd bring him up to the landing and then run down the stairs. He'd follow me to the bottom of them. When he got to the mat he'd slide on it all the way to the front door. Sometimes he banged himself off it. He'd bite me to 'punish' me for causing him to hurt himself. I shouldn't have been playing these kinds of games with him. I knew that now.

'Why didn't you tell me what was happening when I was in London?' I said.

'We knew you wouldn't have agreed,' he said.

I said, 'Every dog is entitled to his first bite. Didn't you often quote that in court when you were in Ballina?'

'This was different,' he said, 'She could have lost her eye.'

I still felt annoyed. There had to be some other way around the problem. Maybe we could have brought him somewhere to have him treated. He could have been tranquillised in some way.

My mother came over with the tea. She put her arms around me. 'I'm sorry,' she said, 'We knew you'd be cut up about it.'

For the next few days I could think of nothing else but Deezer. At the end of the week I dropped out of the Commerce faculty. I entered the Arts one the following day.

I got an exemption in Maths. It was a subject common to both faculties so I only had two subjects to study in my first year instead of three like everyone else.

'So you're reading English now,' my father said to me. He used the Victorian expression that had long gone out of vogue. 'I suppose you'll be out protesting against the government now.'

He should have known I wasn't a political animal. I hardly knew who was even *in* government.

'Don't worry,' I said, 'The hippies have all gone home.' I imagined that included Peter Fonda and Dennis Hopper. It was a pity they hadn't donated their motorbike to me en route.

In a strange way I started to feel Deezer's being put down made my Commerce problem go away. Maybe I wouldn't have to apologise for my changeover to Arts after all.

'You'll be an extra year in university now, won't you?' he said then. I said I would.

'With Hugo there as well,' he said, 'It's going to be hard to keep the wolf from the door. We'll probably end up in the Poor House.'

He often dramatized financial problems. He used to talk to us about people who walked out the windows of the 20th floors of apartment blocks in New York during the Wall Street crash when they lost their fortunes. My mother's attitude was always more casual. It was like 'Que Sera Sera,' from the Doris Day song she loved.

In Ballina, ironically, we'd been worse off . Everyone clubbed together in the Villas. Keith bought a little box one day that he called 'The Kitty.' It had slots for all the different expenses we had. He was meticulous about where everything went. The accountant in him came out at such times.

My father often said, 'Two can live as cheaply as one.' There were actually seven of us in the Villas so that phrase applied many times over. Despite that, he continued to make grim pronouncements about his financial status.

'Money talks,' he used to say, 'Mine said goodbye.' When he talked like that it was difficult to know if he was making a joke of it or not. So many of his statements had that double edge to them.

Some of the family sent him cheques from America. If the envelopes were empty they'd write 'MT' on the outside of them. It became a family joke. 'Read it and weep,' he'd say as he looked at the MT. In reality he didn't mind. Money was a vulgarity. It was 'filthy lucre.'

He told a story about a man who owed him £10. He offered it to him but he didn't want to take it. The man kept throwing it at him and my father kept throwing it back. After a while it became like a game between them.

'What happened eventually?' I asked him.

'I won,' he said. Then he burst out laughing.

What he meant was that he lost. The man ended up with the tenner.

'Wasn't it a good one?' he said as he rocked up and down laughing, 'Be gee wasn't it a good one?' And you had to agree.

Arts

Moving from the stratified world of Commerce to the rough and tumble of Arts felt like getting out of jail. The next three years were like being in Butlin's Holiday Camp. I imagined it was the way my father was in Trinity. The difference was that I passed my exams.

It wasn't like studying. You could talk about D.H. Lawrence all day if you wanted. I couldn't imagine talking about John Maynard Keynes all day.

I'd have wanted to read the books that were on the course anyway – with the exception of 'Beowulf.' We had to do that in the first year. After that it was people like Chaucer. Things improved in the second year. The 'Moderns' appeared on the curriculum. My favourites were the European writers like Brecht and Genet. I didn't talk to my father much about these or even about Irish writers. His orientation was almost totally towards British ones.

He would still be waiting for me when I got home. I was often late. If there was a party on somewhere I might be out half the night. At the weekends I went dancing at the 'Belfield Craze.' Like my father I wasn't much of a dancer but it didn't matter there. Everyone was usually out of their minds with drink. If I didn't go there I settled for the National Ballroom or the Ierne, haunts of displaced culchies like myself who missed the old sod. My father would have preferred me to go the rugby clubs like June did with Audrey, places like Bective and Wesley.

Another place I went sometimes was Sloopy's in D'Olier Street. It always made me feel exotic being there. The ceiling was like the craters of the moon. It also had a pool table. Why was I interested in pool when I should have been chatting to women? If you were lucky you got to do the two things at the same time.

I went to other places like Revolution and Good Time Charlies and Zhivago's. The film 'Dr Zhivago' had been made some years before. I think it was named after that. The film was based on Boris Pasternak's book. We didn't rate him as highly as his Russian counterparts Tolstoy and Dostoevsky in our class in Belfield. He was regarded as a 'one trick pony.' But everyone loved the film, especially for Julie Christie. Why didn't girls who looked like her go to Sloopy's?

At the beginning of 1972 I started going out with a girl who was tall and thin with long black hair parted in the middle like Ali McGraw, who I'd fallen in love with after seeing 'Love Story.' She was a member of the Connolly Youth Movement. I didn't tell my father that. She educated me about Ireland's history under Britain in a way he never did. It wasn't a serious involvement. I can't remember how we broke up. We just drifted apart.

I went to America for the summer. I'd grown up on America – its films, its music, even its politics – so I was looking forward to it. The one thing I wasn't sure I'd be able to handle was the heat. People told me I'd be able to fry an egg on the sidewalks over there.

Basil was staying in a big house in Connecticut. He brought me all over the place during the next few months. I worked at a lot of different jobs – gravedigger, busboy, painter, decorator, demolisher, you name it. At one stage I made plans to go to Las Vegas to see Elvis on stage but they fell through.

I did more things that summer, it seemed, than I'd done in my entire life up to this. There was always something happening. How could life in Dublin ever measure up to it? I saw the film 'Easy Rider' one night. Jack Nicholson had a great line in it as he sat round a campfire with Peter Fonda and Dennis Hopper smoking pot, 'This used to be a helluva country once.'

To me it still was. I came back to Ireland with an obsession that I'd get an Easy Rider motorbike like Fonda and Hopper drove in the film, one of the ones with the wide handlebars. I was brought back to earth when I learned that they weren't on sale in the country. If they were they'd probably have cost a king's ransom.

The film blew my mind. I don't know if my father ever saw it. I read somewhere that it caused tension between Peter Fonda and his own father, Henry, who was a pillar of the establishment. My father was hardly that but anytime I talked about it I could see a strange expression on his face. Maybe he was worried that I might start wearing flowers in my hair and go off to a hippie commune somewhere.

Back at Belfield the books on our courses got more interesting. Gone were the bad old days of 'Beowulf' and Chaucer. I enjoyed reading them so much I found myself not wanting to graduate. I said to him one day, 'I think I know how you felt at Trinity.' He said, 'I hated the books I had to read. It was what I did between lectures that kept me there so long.'

I went to Washington after finishing Second Arts. Audrey and Jacinta were there. They were staying in an apartment block. Audrey was well in with the man who managed it. She'd given his wife some medical treatment once. Her association with him resulted in me getting a job as a janitor in the building. I wasn't supposed to be staying in it. It would have pushed up Audrey and Jacinta's rent if he knew.

He was amazed at how early I made it into work every day. 'How did you get across the city so fast?' he'd say. The truth of the matter was that I just took the lift down a few floors to Reception – or the 'elevator,' as they said.

Audrey was nursing in a hospital in the city. It was called the Walter Reed. Jacinta was dating a man called Dan. He worked there. Audrey was dating his room-mate.

My parents dressed up for a function

Washington was a fascinating city. There were lots of things to do. One day I visited the Smithsonian Institute and saw the moon rock. It brought me back to four years before when I'd looked at it on television. Now it was just inches away from me.

I met Aunt Valerie's daughter, who was also called Valerie, later on that summer. It was on a trip I made to New York in the middle of it. She was another lady living in virtual poverty. All the Valeries and all the poverty.

Why did pure people fare so badly in life? Why did unlikeable people thrive?

Valerie had a son called George. Clive was studying in Fordham University that year. He managed to get George into a course there. He was all set for a great career but he died young in yet another tragedy. Yet another beautiful soul had bitten the dust.

Relationship

In the autumn I met Mary, the woman who would eventually become my wife. She was working in a solicitor's office at the time. I met her at a party in the appropriately named Bird Avenue. Her name was appropriate too when I thought of how many of my grandfather's wives were called Mary.

She said she liked my green eyes. Her own ones were blue. She said her mother always dressed her in blue to match them when she was a little girl. As a result she took a turn against that colour. She preferred wearing green now. I said anything was okay but red.

I never liked red. She said girls liked to wear red dresses at dances. They thought it would give them a better chance of being asked out onto the floor. I couldn't understand that. I always avoided girls in red, especially blood red. I said my colour scheme for women was the same as for traffic: Green for Go and Red for Stop.

After the night in Bird Avenue we started meeting once a week. It was usually outside a shop on the Quays called Demesne Products. We'd go for a drink or to the pictures. After we got to know one another better I brought her out to the Villas. My father took to her immediately. They had a lot to talk about because of her being involved in the legal world.

'He made me feel a part of the family from the first day I met him,' she said to me. She also thought nobody could tell a story like he could. We all tried to but the harder we tried, the more we failed to measure up. You either had it or you didn't. She saw how he 'became' the story he was telling, or the joke or the recitation. There was no difference between the teller and the tale.

I was writing some educational guides for the Inter Cert and Leaving Cert at the time. Mary typed them up for me.

'She's my secretary as well as my girlfriend,' I said to him.

'Your amanuensis,' he corrected.

I also introduced her to the rest of the family. There were so many of us it can't have been easy for her. Her own family only had three in it. She said her world was very ordered in comparison to ours. There were people coming and going at all hours in Norfolk. She saw our life as being like a continuous party.

My father told her a lot of stories about his family tree. I watched her kick off her shoes and settle into the couch as he told her about my grandfather's three wives, his achievements in Ballina, the way he built up his fortune.

He dredged his memory banks to unearth stories he hadn't told in over a decade, stories involving people long dead before I was born. As I listened to him talking it seemed to me that they were more real to him, and maybe by extension to Mary, than stories of the living.

She took everything in much better than I ever did. I always found it hard to get interested in people I'd never met even if they were my relations. Why should I have cared? Even if you had blue blood somewhere in your heritage it wasn't always there. If you went back far enough we'd all have been climbing trees.

One day I was in Aunt Florence's house in Dun Laoghaire when a man sat beside me that I didn't know. 'What's your relationship to her?' I said to him. 'I'm her son!" he spluttered.

Mary learned so much about my background at this time that it became a source of amusement to me. I said to her one day that if I wanted to find out something about my background I'd ask her for details. 'It's all there for you if you want it,' she said, 'He'd love you to be more interested.'

I wished I could be but it just wasn't in me. I told her I was never going to be a genealogist. I was more like the Hollywood aristocrat who boasted about being able to trace his ancestry all the way back to his father.

Many of his stories concerned drinking in Ballina. She wasn't surprised by them. Her father's job involved travelling around the country examining weights and measures in shops.

Her mother always hated when he had to go to Ballina. She knew it had a reputation as a drinking town. I thought nothing of all the bars I saw when I was growing up. When you're young you think everything you see is the norm. It was only when I got older and went to other places I realised how disproportionate the spread was in relation to Ballina. No wonder we turned out so many alcoholics.

I sat in on my father's chats with Mary even when my mind was elsewhere. He always loved an audience. If one of us left the room in the middle of a story he'd stop until we came back. We both had to hear every word.

Mary became as much of a D-M as the rest of us over time but there were still differences in the way the two of us lived. That was made clear to me the night she came round to the Villas when the clocks were supposed to have been put back. We'd forgotten to do that.

'They're all saying the wrong time,' she said.

'Nobody bothers much about that kind of thing here,' I told her.

She had a cuckoo clock in her house that chirped on the hour. That would have driven me mad. She liked how different we were. If you ever came to the Malones she said, you could be sure you'd miss the last bus home. She often did. I drove her home on Basil's Honda 50 sometimes but I was often too tired for that and she'd end up staying overnight. It meant going into work from the Villas the next morning.

We weren't sleeping together but sometimes I lay on the bed with her outside the clothes before she went to sleep. One night my father walked in on us. It was in the middle of the night. He turned on the light. We were just talking but he thought there was something else going on. He stopped for a second when he saw us. I saw the monocle going in. He said, 'Has anyone seen *The Irish Times* ?' I thought it was classic. It was so him. He was probably trying not to embarrass us. We used to laugh about it afterwards.

I started writing film reviews now. There was no outlet for them in UCD. Instead I did them for a Trinity magazine, 'TCD Miscellany.' It was my first time seeing my name in print. There was no money for it but it was a buzz. The terror of the blank page that used to hit me when I was faced with Muredach's essays was gone now. That was because I was enjoying what I was doing. It wasn't like pulling teeth to string the sentences together.

The first film I reviewed was a Dirk Bogarde one, 'The Night Porter.' I used as many big words as I could in it. Maybe I was trying to impress my father. He liked the fact that it was a Trinity magazine.

I used to go in to TCD to deliver my copy. Walking across the cobblestones gave me the kind of buzz he must have had all those years before. Trinity had an excitement about it that Belfield never could approximate to. Maybe it was because the campus was so near to everything. It was part of the city and yet separate from it. It reeked of antiquity and yet was intensely modern.

So why hadn't I gone there myself? Probably because I thought I'd be punching above my weight in it. I'd have had the same sense of awkwardness I had in Belvedere, or with the posh people of Ballina, or with southside Dubliners. That was ironic because Belfield was closer to Dublin 4 than Trinity.

He used to say to me after reading my reviews, 'You sound like you swallowed the dictionary.' I told him it wasn't off the ground I licked it. It was like a role reversal from the days he used to do my essays for me in Muredach's. Now he was learning words from me instead of the other way round.

He'd never have gone to a film like 'The Night Porter.' Hugo would. He became the person I talked to most about films now. Norfolk was still a night owl's house. We often stayed up well after midnight talking about films like this that my father would have had no interest in. If he joined us, our focus shifted.

Audrey was working in a hospital in Palmerstown now. It was a long drive out to it. Some of her shifts started at dawn. She needed her sleep. So did my mother and June, the two other people living in the house. Sometimes Hugo and myself would still be up as they were getting ready to go to work.

Hugo played Bob Dylan songs on his guitar, or his 'hurdy gurdy' as my father called it. I was a big fan of Dylan too.

If we stayed up all night I'd leave notes for my mother saying something like 'Call me at 2. I have a lecture.'

Hugo made burnt toast as we talked nonsense about Dylan or the meaning of life. Neither of us were exactly style gurus at the time. I had a woolly jumper that was held together by holes like a fishing net. Hugo was usually dressed in a pair of grey bell bottoms that were getting ready to walk off him.

Philosophy was my second subject with English. It was his too. We felt important using the word 'Existential' even though we hadn't the foggiest what it meant. It was amusing listening to Hugo trying to get my father in on Jean-Paul Sartre.

There was no way that was ever going to happen. Hugo would say something like, 'This is a revolutionary philosophy.' My father would reply, 'There's nothing new under the sun. I'd prefer to talk about how many angels can dance on the head of a pin.'

Hugo also talked about another existentialist, Albert Camus. He talked mainly about his book 'The Outsider.' He'd read it in All Hallows and it changed his life. It changed mine too.

The idea of a man being put to death because he couldn't grieve for his mother blew my mind. I shared Camus' sense of the absurd sometimes. My father did too even if he didn't use that word. Hugo and myself trotted out the trendy phrases about existentialism that we listened to in Theatre L but my father lived them.

We felt superior to him when we talked about Camus or Sartre, or about film stars like Marlon Brando or James Dean. Dean said to his father in *Rebel Without a Cause*, 'You don't understand me!' his words speaking to a generation, Generation X. I fancied myself as being a member of that.

We also felt superior to him when we were talking about Dylan. I don't think he ever listened to a Dylan song in his life. 'Are you two intending to become hippies?' he said to us one night when we were singing one of his songs, if you could call warbling out of tune at 3 a.m. singing. All pop singers were lumped into that category for him. Maybe he was thinking back to how much I went on about 'Easy Rider' after coming back from Connecticut.

I could never be a hippie because I was never able to wear my hair long. It was too curly. Now and again I wet it. I sellotaped it to the side of my face to try and give myself locks but after I peeled off the sellotape the hair just flared out again.

Sometimes before going to bed, Hugo and myself would go into my father's room to continue the chats. He still loved talking about the past. I told him I had no time for it. Maybe I was like all young people. J felt above it and everything it represented.

Eamon De Valera arrived out to the campus one day for some function or other. He was in his nineties at the time. To me he was like a relic. He'd dominated my youth in politics just like John Charles McQuaid did in religion. They were like two sides of the one coin, two people who wanted to keep us mired in tradition. I was desperate to get away from that. Having said that, I couldn't remember my father talking much about either of them. One of them was too nationalistic. The other didn't have the aura he expected from church leaders.

There wasn't much in his bedroom besides a bed and a television. This was his world, lying on one and watching the other. I didn't know how anyone's existence could be this basic. It felt like a cave to me sometimes. One winter we got a Super Ser for him for heat. It had gas canisters that we replaced every time they were empty.

I often lay on the bed with him. He'd cut out articles from the paper and show them to me. 'What do you think of that?' he'd say. It would usually be an item about something that happened that day, an unusual event or maybe something to do with the law, a case that wasn't contested properly or someone who escaped jail on a technicality. 'People are getting away with murder nowadays,' he'd say, 'Literally.' It was the old chestnut. If it had an air I could have sung it.

He had a bell he used to ring for tea like he did in Ballina. It had a round white top on it. There was a little button he pressed whenever he wanted a cup. It was as if he was royalty. My mother had no problem with that.

'I think I'll have another one, Pat,' he'd say. She never complained. The bottomless cup was still on the range. 'You haven't lived in vain!' he'd say when she brought it in.

The idea of him lending a hand in the kitchen was unthinkable. I don't think anyone in the family ever considered such a prospect, least of all my mother. Apart from the fact that he'd probably have poisoned the lot of us, including himself, there was also the possibility that he'd set the house up.

A group decision was made soon after we got to the Villas that he was never to be let loose anywhere near the Aga. He was aware of its existence and may even have taken a teapot off it once in a blue moon but I doubt he knew of any other functions it could perform.

We kept him away from the pressure cooker as well. One day someone left the top of it loose. It flew through the kitchen window and into the glasshouse, practically decapitating the people sitting there at the time. If this wasn't a disincentive to someone like him cooking something in it I don't know what was. From an early stage of the marriage I think my mother decided that the kitchen would be off limits to him except at a safe hour when everyone was watered and fed. At such times he could venture into it to entertain those of us still in Ireland with stories about his past, preferably at a safe distance from anything hot.

Ruth had also left Ireland by now. She met an American man, John, at a do in the American Embassy one night and they got serious with one another very soon. Before she knew where she was he was talking about marriage. She said yes and then he went into my father to ask for her hand. It was a Victorian gesture and it impressed him.

'I thought that sort of thing had gone out,' he said.

They got married soon afterwards. I was away at the time. Someone told me my mother popped a Valium into

John's mouth when he was on his way to the church. She hadn't changed. It was still the panacea for all forms of nerves in her book.

We used to joke that she'd give you one for everything from a pain in your big toe to heart disease. You hardly even needed a prescription for them. Dr Igoe doled them out to her like jellybeans. It was like, 'Take two, they're small. Maybe put a bit of salt on to sweeten.' It was the white 2 milligram ones for small stresses and the yellow 5 mg for big ones. Seriously disturbed people got the Big Casino 10 mg blue ones. These were liable to make you sleep through a hurricane.

Keith was married now as well. He was 33 when he finally took the plunge with Jacqueline. 'The age of J.C. himself when he died,' he said ominously.

He was happy with Jacqueline in their house in Artane but he spent a lot of time in the Villas. I had a friend called Dermot who dropped in sometimes. Keith seemed to be there every time he called.

'I thought Keith was married,' he said to me one day. I said, 'He is. He just needs time to get used to the idea.' We used to joke that if Jacqueline wanted to find out how he was, she'd have to ring my mother.

Norfolk was such a womb, it was difficult for any of us to leave it, married or not.

Suited, as ever, on Enniscrone beach

Gambler

Even though my father wasn't in Uncle Michael's league as regards betting, reading the racing pages formed a large part of his day. He liked telling the story of a man who went into a bookie's office one day and said to the cashier, 'I have a feeling I'm going to win today.' She replied, 'That's the feeling that keeps us in business.'

On Grand National Day he'd close his eyes and stick a pin on the page where the horses' names were. Otherwise he'd put a shilling each way on about fifty different horses. He'd get worked up if there was a dead heat or a steward's enquiry. I could never understand it considering the bets were so small.

He used to place them over the phone. The women in the bookie's offices must have been tearing their hair out at the number of horses involved. The calls used to go on for ages. Sometimes they'd have to put him on 'Hold' as they attended other customers.

He was impatient if they delayed him. My mother used to say, 'You'll be there for the two days.' It was her way of saying 'a long time.' One day after he was kept waiting for a few minutes longer than usual he said to the girl on the other end of the line, 'Did you enjoy your holidays?'

'You're very smart.' she snapped back.

Another day I heard him saying to one of the staff, 'Did you speak or did my ears flap?'

One of the horses he followed was called Uncle Whiskers. I use the word 'followed' advisedly. 'The horses I follow,' as Frank Sinatra said once, 'follow the horses.' Uncle Whiskers must have been on the old age pension, or whatever the horse equivalent of that was.

He never won a race in his life but my father kept backing him every time he saw his name. 'I can't let him go,' he'd say, 'I'd never forgive myself if he won.'

There was hardly any danger of that. 'He wasn't an also ran,' we used to joke, 'He was an also walked.' My father became increasingly frustrated every time he ended up 'down the field.' I never knew why because he'd only have put buttons on him.

He backed less horses than before as the seventies went on, transferring his attention to us. He became more attentive to us, more curious about what we were doing with our days.

He'd been protective of us as children but he got worse now. If any of us had a run-in with someone we were afraid to tell him in case he got involved. It was like when he wrote the letters in Ballina that I didn't post. If we started some story about a problem we were having with anyone, my mother would put her hand over her mouth to gesture us to stop.

Her attitude was diametrically opposed to his. She adhered to the Doris Day sentiment of 'Que Sera Sera' from her song, or a similar one from The Beatles, 'Let it Be.' If I told her about a problem I was having she'd quote the chorus of a song from 'West Side Story' called 'Cool': 'Got a rocket in your pocket, keep cool lickle boy.'

My father worried anytime one of us had a health problem. Hugo had a slipped disc. Basil put his hand through a pane of glass one day in Joan O'Reilly's house before he went to America. Jacinta had a fall stepping onto a bus with a typewriter. Ruth got hit in the head by a golf ball on a pitch and putt course. It wasn't a serious injury but he treated it like one.

Ruth was dating a man who had epilepsy at the time. He worried about that too. The man drove a car. What if he got a fit when she was in it with him?

June got a marriage proposal from a Welshman. He didn't want her moving out of Ireland with him. Luckily, June felt the same and stayed put.

One night when I was coming home from a Boy Scouts event I was at with Mary in the Devil's Glen it started to rain. She was on the back of my motorbike at the time. By now I'd traded in Basil's Honda 50 for a Yamaha twin. We skidded and came off it, careering into a ditch. Mary escaped unhurt as she was wearing the single helmet we had but I got cut on the forehead.

I was bleeding a lot but I didn't have myself stitched up. Because it was raining I thought it was rain instead of blood. I was too tired to look at myself in the mirror when I got home. I went to bed as soon as I went in the door and promptly fell asleep. The next morning my forehead was stuck to the pillow with coagulated blood. My father nearly had a seizure when he saw me.

He worried about all these kinds of things much more than he used to. We tried to tell him about as few of them as we could.

I thought his problem was that he had too much time to think. It made him obsess on details. His diary was like a logbook. He put everything into it, things like where we were all going on a given day – to jobs, social events, even down to the shops.

Despite him saying he didn't want to see visitors I wondered if he was lonely. Sometimes when someone came to the house he'd latch on to them as if he hadn't seen anyone for months.

We had a friend called Donie O'Donoghue. He'd dated Jacinta when she was in Ireland and he was also a great friend of June's. He'd started life being a band manager and then became an accountant. He was now studying law to become a barrister.

My father engaged him in lengthy discussions about complicated legal cases. Sometimes they stayed up talking half the night. Donie had an intricate mind. He loved these kinds of conversations. My father gave him many of his law books as gifts afterwards.

Donie always had something funny to say to me whenever he saw me. One day when he was in the middle of a discussion with my father about some knotty point of the law he said to me, 'I suppose you're going to tell me I don't exist.'

He didn't practice much as a barrister. It was just something he did to stimulate a mind that was always on fire. He did some accountancy on the side and made good money at it.

He told me once that I should have stuck at it instead of going into the world of Arts.

'You'd have been as rich as Croesus,' he said.

'No,' I said, 'More likely I'd have been six feet under from boredom.'

That wasn't to say English was always good. After coming through 'Beowulf' and 'Chaucer' I had a honeymoon period with it but then it got dense again. In our last year we had to study something called Structuralism, which chopped texts up into little pieces and analysed them to the death. It bored me just as much as Accountancy did. I felt like saying to the lecturer, 'If I was that interested in structure I'd have gone into the architecture department.'

In fact the whole idea of analysing literature had always seemed anathema to me. It was like analysing breathing. So why did I register for an academic course in it? I couldn't answer that. I just wanted to read books.

Graduation

My father turned seventy in 1974. He was, as he put it, 'Three score and ten,' the Biblical span. I got my B.A. that year too. I should have left Belfield after I got it but I didn't. Instead of going out into the world I signed up for an M.A. in English.

It involved writing an 18,000 word thesis on an author of my choice. Keith thought I should do it on F. Scott Fitzgerald. My father wanted that as well. Both of them liked the magical world of the Jazz Era that Fitzgerald conjured up. I thought of myself more as a realist so I chose Ernest Hemingway instead.

There was a famous exchange that took place between Hemingway and Fitzgerald once. Fitzgerald said to Hemingway, 'The rich are different from you and me.' Hemingway replied, 'Yes, they have more money.'

My father had lived like Fitzgerald in Trinity. Keith would have liked to. Hemingway was fascinated by that world for a while when he was consorting with Fitzgerald's friends Gerald and Sara Murphy. He grew bored with it eventually, writing about this in his story 'The Snows of Kilimanjaro.'

It never lost its allure for Fitzgerald, even after the Jazz Era ended and his own life went to hell. Maybe none of us ever change our dispositions no matter what life does to us. My father would have continued dreaming he dwelt in Marble Hall even if, like Uncle Michael, he lived in a tenement.

He was like Hemingway in his temperament. Both of them were larger than life and both were jovial in company. But Hemingway wasn't one of his favourite authors. He liked the sweep of his novels but not the tight-lipped tone of his stories.

He also had problems with him politically, seeing him as a communist as a result of his escapades during the Spanish Civil War. Communism was a word he whispered as much as cancer. He feared 'the hammer and sickle.'

'Hemingway was left wing, wasn't he?' he said. It was meant as a criticism. He asked me if I was that way too. He'd deduced as much from some of my outpourings over the years. I said I didn't see things in terms of right and left but rather right and wrong.

My thesis concerned Hemingway's literary style. It was as dull as ditchwater. The university gave me a bound copy of it which I lost. That was probably for the best. Putting an author I liked into an academic straitjacket was never going to be a good idea.

My father was a relief from the whole ambience surrounding the M.A. There was rarely a spontaneous reaction to books there. All too often it was pseudo-intellectuals spouting cliches about the same critics, people like R.P. Blackmur, Lionel Trilling, Roland Barthes. He knew none of these people and he was better off.

At the tutorials the sense of preciousness got even worse. People nurtured their theses like babies. They talked coyly about subjects like The Omniscient Perspective of the Nineteenth Century Narrator when all I wanted to do was turn pages of books. At such times I gravitate towards him for a dose of reality, an escape from there eunuchs on the literary harem.

Despite such disenchantment, I tinkered around with the idea of doing a Ph.D. for a while after getting the M.A. It would have meant a further two years in Belfield.

'You'll have half the alphabet after your name before you're finished,' he said to me.

He wanted me to attend the graduation ceremony for the M.A. I told him I'd prefer to fly under the radar.

‘You’re the one who deserves the credit,’ I said, ‘You paid the fees. All I did was read a few books.’ He couldn’t understand my attitude. We were like chalk and cheese.

‘You’re too quiet,’ he said, ‘If you don’t ring the bell on your bike no one else will.’

He told me a joke about a man who went to a psychologist suffering from an inferiority complex. The psychologist examined him. Then he said, ‘I’ve examined your case and I’ve come to a conclusion. You don’t have a complex. You’re just inferior.’ He went into hysterics when he told that one.

‘Win your spurs and wear them,’ he said.

I never liked doing that. I’d read a book when I was in UCD called ‘I’m Okay, You’re Okay.’ Surprise surprise, it was written by an American.

I had no problem with the ‘You’re okay’ part but a lot of the time I felt I wasn’t okay myself. I knew some Americans whose attitude was, ‘I’m okay, you’re not okay.’

Maybe I was the opposite. It was like the difference between the two continents. My father said he knew a man in Ballina once who, as he put it, apologised for being alive. He didn’t want me to be like that.

‘Don’t criticise yourself,’ he said, ‘There are enough people who’ll do that for you.’ It went back to the thing about his father, about his need to stand firm against people who wanted to pull him down.

I was writing some stories for David Marcus’ page in the ‘Irish Press’ at this time. So was Mary. Her father kept her ones in his wallet to show off to people. My father didn’t know what to make of mine.

I was writing some poems too at this time. For some reason these meant more to him. I had a poem published in Marcus’ page one Saturday that he liked. He encouraged me to do more of them. ‘Many great men lived before Agamemnon,’ he said, ‘but died for the want of a poet to sing their praises.' This was a bit lofty considering my poem was about coming home to a cold water flat after a night out boozing.

He didn't keep my stories in his wallet like Mary's father did. Instead it was filled with photographs of the family. Whenever he was in a pub in Ballina he used to take them out to show to people. Usually the sight of them caused a stampede for the exit. 'I could clear a bar,' he'd say.

Mary wrote less than me but she had a better strike rate with Marcus. Sometimes I tried too hard. Her words flowed out of her more freely. I told her she should write more stories.

'I can only do them when they come to me,' she said, 'Otherwise it doesn't work.'

I tried to force mine. Maybe I was already thinking of a career in writing. For her it was just a hobby, something to fill in the time when nothing was happening at work. She stuffed pages into her typewriter and let the stories come out as they would. When she was at home, for some reason, she didn't do as many. She worked better with noise around her. I liked the noise of the typewriter but I wouldn't have been able to write with people around me.

Eventually Marcus stopped taking my stories. His change of attitude made me lose heart. I felt he'd lit a fire in me and now he was dousing it. I might have been better if he'd never taken anything I sent him. Then I wouldn't have been, as they said, bitten by the bug.

My father told me not to worry, that I'd get other ones accepted by him in the future.

'His opinion doesn't mean something isn't good,' he said, 'He's only one person. Keep at it and you'll get there.' I wasn't sure if he was being falsely polite. He was obviously prejudiced. If I wrote 'The cat sat on the mat,' he'd have been in ecstacies about it.

His words consoled me. I was vulnerable at this time. Maybe every young writer is. We think everything we write is going to stop the world. Then someone says, 'This is no good,' and we go to pieces.

He told me a joke about a writer who was depressed because his editor condensed his autobiography into a short story. I think the point was that he took himself too seriously.

He had another story about a writer who couldn't get off the ground. No matter how hard he tried, he kept getting rejection slips. Eventually he had enough to wallpaper his study. But he wouldn't lie down. He kept sending material to an editor. With one submission he wrote to him, 'If you don't like this, don't worry. I have other irons in the fire.' The editor wrote back, 'Put it with the other irons.'

I thought I was spending too much time concentrating on writing. After a certain time that had a counter-productive effect. I was living in a kind of cloud cuckoo land, a limbo between education and life.

In some ways I was a writer in search of a theme, someone with more perspiration than inspiration. There was nothing wrong with a work ethic but it had to be backed up with experience. I hadn't been blooded enough in life. It meant a lot of my stories were woolly. Marcus had mentioned the purple patches in them when I was sending him almost one a week, not to mention all the stream-of-consciousness poems on the side. Maybe it was time to stand back from them and do some living before I put pen to paper again.

Against my father's wished I stayed away from the graduation ceremony, going down to the Botanical Gardens instead and having a few photos of myself taken by family members, trying to look as intelligent as I could in my handmade mortarboard and gown.

My father looked at me proudly. I wondered if he was thinking of his own graduation all those years ago in Trinity, of how his life had gone since. It would have been almost forty years ago to the day. Where would I be in forty years, I wondered.

I didn't think of life after graduation. Other people in my class surveyed their options in advertising, or broadcasting in RTE. For me the degree was an end in itself.

I didn't know what job I wanted to go into. The M.A. had mainly been to buy thinking time for myself. I was like my father in Trinity, wrapping myself in a place where I could read books without having to think of putting them to any practical use. Gainful employment was something to be feared, an entry into a world I dreaded as much as Muredach's when I went there first.

My father asked me what I wanted to do. Teaching was a possibility, I told him, but I wasn't sure I'd be good at it. He knew I liked children. Having them in your face every day of the week might be a different proposition.

To stave of the evil world of employment a while longer I decided to go to Europe for a few months. He was fine about that. 'Spread your wings,' he said, 'You'll be working long enough.'

He'd never been out of Ireland himself. That didn't seem to bother him. Nobody was shoving foreign travel in people's faces in those days like they do now. He was hardly aware of it.

He often spoke of people with 'travelled bodies and untravelled minds.' I knew what he meant. People told you they were going somewhere exotic and you knew by the way they said it that they thought it made them exotic too. The truth was that they were as boring abroad as they were at home, maybe even more so. No matter where you went, you still had to pack yourself.

My mother had never been abroad either. I couldn't imagine them going on a holiday together anywhere, especially overseas. They wouldn't have known what to do. As my mother said, the only holidays she ever had was having babies. I never remember seeing my father with anything approaching a tan. Such things belonged to a future era. Irishmen of his generation preferred to say, 'I don't tan, I rust.'

I flew to Paris with a classmate, a friend of a friend from another faculty. One night in a cinema on the Champs-Elysses we saw a John Wayne film. Hearing Wayne's voice dubbed into French by a man who sounded like Bela Lugosi was an experience I wouldn't forget in a hurry.

We hitched from Paris to Athens on flimsy resources. Some nights we slept in doorways. Other times we used petrol stations and fields. There were nights where we even slept on the sides of roads. I don't know how we weren't killed. Trucks used to plough by at the rate of knots.

These were the most carefree months of my life, maybe because I knew they were the last ones I'd have without some sort of responsibility hanging over me – the responsibility of a job, of having to earn money, to rise to a clock. Because of that I savoured them.

Each dawn became precious. Even listening to birds singing did because they were doing it in different countries to my own one. We did odd jobs to earn a few pounds but most of the time we spent examining our navels. Students are good at that.

One night I slept on a beach. It was romantic, something I'd never have done in Ireland. One day when I was hitch-hiking a man went out of his way to bring me where I wanted to go.

'I did something like you're doing when I was your age,' he said, 'Maybe when you're my age you'll do something like this for someone else.'

I told him I hoped I would. I promised myself I'd never grow old enough not to want to.

We were home by Christmas. I was still none the wiser about how I was going to spend my future.

'Well,' my father said, 'How did you get on?'

'I had the time of my life,' I said.

'Good,' he said, 'You deserved it.'

The unasked question hung in the air like, as he might have put it, the sword of Damocles: what was I going to do to earn a crust?

The answer was as far away from me as it would ever be. I was still no closer to finding out how I might evade the possibility of signing my autograph in the dole office in Gardiner Street for the rest of my natural.

I found myself wondering if Room Number 9 in Trinity was still available. Maybe my father and myself could move into it fulltime and watch the girls gallivanting up and down Grafton Street from the railings.

Work

I did some night security work for pin money over the next few months. It was never going to be anything more than a stopgap.

The elephant in the room was the dreaded C word – Career. Which one was I going to choose? I put on my thinking cap and looked at the options. None of them looked any better than they had before I went to Greece.

Just as I was running out of ideas, an Education Minister called John Wilson set up a scheme where disaffected graduates like myself could do a one-year course in Pat's Training college that allowed us to become Primary School teachers. In the absence of any other opportunity I went for it. So did a few other work-shy wannabes I was hanging around with.

The usual course was three years so I was getting something concrete out of the Arts degree after all. I got to squash Maths when I shifted from Commerce to Arts. Now I was getting a whole two years off. It seemed that every U-turn I made in life had at least some compensatory factor attached to it. It was all about playing the system if you were used to 'the good life.'

Some of my equally pampered classmates looked down on the B. Ed people.

'They've only read books by educational psychologists,' they said, not the 'heavy hitters' like Sartre and Camus that we were up to our tonsils with.

Some of the B.Eds looked down on us as well, thinking we were going into teaching not so much for a vocation but a vacation.

Maybe they were right. Who'd say no to a job that gave you over three months a year holidays? And why would someone who had a craving to work with kids sign up for a course in English and Philosophy? We might as well have been studying horticulture as far as the children of the nation were concerned.

My father wasn't impressed at my decision.

'I can't see you in front of a group of children,' he said to me.

'That makes two of us,' I said.

He wasn't over the moon about any of his children becoming teachers, even Hugo, but Secondary ranked significantly higher in his eyes than Primary. He told me he dated a Primary Teacher once and found her to be 'common.'

She was also, he said, on the make. 'She wanted to marry up,' was the way he put it. When he saw her for what she was he broke it off with her.

She became involved with another man soon afterwards. He thought it was 'on the rebound' from him. He said he could imagine her playing hard to get. 'He chased her till she caught him,' was the way he put it.

I told him I was no keener on Primary Teaching than he was but I had to get some kind of a job. I knew he wasn't going to like it any more than he liked me going to UCD. Someone said to him once that 'NT' stood for 'National Tramp' instead of National Teacher. It was a view he shared.

By the time I started in Pat's his nerves were getting at him more.

One day he starting talking about dying.

'I'm coming up the straight,' he said.

It was sad to hear him saying something like that.

I told him he could have a lot of years left if he minded himself but he didn't want to hear that kind of talk.

'We kill time,' he said, 'and then time kills us.'

He started quoting some lines from Omar Khayyam's 'Rubaiyat':

'The moving finger writes
And having writ moves on
Nor all thy piety not wit
Shall lure it back to cancel half a line
Nor all thy tears wash out a word of it.'

He spoke about the past as if it was yesterday. The 'real' yesterday, in contrast, was forgotten. He found himself remembering things that took place twenty years before better than he could things that happened twenty minutes ago.

'Memory is the only friend that grief can call its own,' he used to say. It became yet another of his mantras, yet another phrase you could sing if it had an air to it.

I felt his main problem was that he had too much time to think. The rest of us talked about what we were doing in our work, or in my case what we were about to do.

We talked about music, films, sports. He wasn't really 'into' any of these things. He got involved in the political world to a degree but not as much as before and usually negatively.

He spent most of his time going through old papers that he'd kept from the Ballina days.

In some ways he was like a character from Beckett. 'I take them out in the morning,' he'd say, 'and put them back in the same order at night.'

It was sad watching him. No matter how much the activity engaged him, it was eventually going to reach saturation point. When it did, he put them away. I thought that might lead to him immersing himself in other things but it didn't.

There was nothing to fill the vacuum. Left without them he just gazed into the middle distance from his bed, only vaguely aware of the television humming away in the background.

'Life has passed me by,' he'd say. I'd try to console him, telling him he had my mother and all of us and the television and the newspapers. He'd give out to himself for complaining but there were times all these things meant nothing to him.

'Why don't you go into town?' I said to him one day. He usually dressed himself up if he was doing that.

'What would be the point?' he said, 'Who would I see?' He gave out about people invading his privacy but then, inversely, seemed to miss them.

I wished there was some way he could be distracted from himself. Drink had done that once. Nobody wanted to see him going back to it.

It wouldn't have meant anything to him anyway now. It was tied up with his lifestyle at the time, the lifestyle of a world that could never come again. My mother certainly didn't miss it. I thought of her words, 'It was like a match to a flame.' Without it he was happier but in some ways less himself.

The side of him that reminded me of Beckett spilled over into some of his musings.

'You might as well be happy today,' he used to say, 'because things will probably be worse tomorrow.'

'The only time I feel good,' he said to me one day, 'is when I get bored of being bored.' Then he started laughing. It was the way with a lot of his pronouncements. Once he got them out of himself they didn't seem to apply to him anymore.

Sometimes I didn't know if he said things like that out of a grim sense of fun. He'd look at you to see would you laugh. When that was the case I didn't feel too bad for him. It was as if he was outside himself looking in, treating

My mother

himself as a character from some play he was making up for light relief.

Maybe Beckett was a bit like that too. His writing was like an ode to misery but many critics said he was a comedian in disguise. The real depressives, I thought, were too depressed to write about their condition.

The happiest people in the world, my father said, were the ones in mental homes, people who wandered up and down corridors thinking they were Napoleon. 'It's the rest of us I feel sorry for,' he said, 'The so-called sane ones.'

'We're born and we die,' he said to me one day, 'In between, if we're lucky, we have some fun. Happiness is a thing called Joe.' It was chilling listening to the way he could say so much in so few words. He dropped phrases like acid. Playwrights who were lauded from the rooftops for their bleak wisdom could have taken a leaf out of his book. He was more profound than many of the ones I was studying for a course called Theatre of the Absurd. I'd reply to him with cliches like, 'Don't be so negative' or 'You'll feel better tomorrow.' But he usually did. Getting the frustration out took it away. The next day he'd be telling some joke from a Three Stooges film or a Laurel and Hardy one. I remembered reading somewhere that a literary critic said to Beckett once of the two hoboes from 'Waiting for Godot,' 'They speak as if they've been to university.' Beckett replied, 'How do you know they haven't?'

I felt a lot of my father's gloomy pronouncements were a result of him being out of his work situation. Inactivity affected his morale. I told him nobody could be at the top of the tree all the time. When you were on the lower branches it was important to realise that. Maybe you could even pretend you were still on the top one. He'd done that when we came to Dublin first. If we practised mind control we could all be Napoleons in our minds, like the people he talked about in the mental homes. We could all see Elba.

I wanted to tell him I understood him, that I shared his sense of lostness, but people didn't talk to their fathers like that then. There were designated roles between parents and children. I wanted to cut through them but I didn't know how. Even though there was a generation between us, in fact two generations, I didn't feel a generation 'gap.'

If he was younger and from a different time I might have sat on his shoulders watching Bohemians play soccer matches in Dalymount Park. It was near us.

Sometimes I saw fathers with their sons on the street near it. I used to think they looked so near in age they might have been brothers. For a minute I might be envious. But then I'd think: I already had brothers. A father should be different.

Someone said to me once, 'Your father is old enough to be your grandfather.' I said, 'So what?' It never felt like that because he was so young at heart. When he was in one of his silly moods I almost felt as if I was the older one. 'A little nonsense now and then,' he'd say, 'is treasured by the best of men.'

When he was in good form, all the family felt good too. It was as if the sun was shining all day. But when he was down we felt down too. He didn't want us to be. It was his personality. He had such a large one it took over everything. Like the king in fairytales, when he laughed we laughed and when he cried we cried.

Or maybe we just went quiet. That was my mother's reaction. It had to be. Otherwise she'd have used up all her laughter and tears over the years. She kept her emotional batteries on 'Charge' all the time. It meant that she seemed able for anything life threw at her. It wasn't that she didn't care about how my father oscillated. She cared more than any of us. But she had to be above it in some way to deal with it. 'Everything will be all right,' she'd say. And it usually was.

Many nights he sat up into the small hours reading newspapers in bed, tearing articles out of them for us to read. I don't know how my mother slept through that. She'd gotten used to sleeping with the light on over the years. It was her 'abnormal normal.' She never complained even if her eyes were falling out of her head the next morning.

Every Sunday he bought the English paper, 'The People.' 'I know it's a rag,' he'd say by way of excusing it. People talked of it being a pagan publication because of its Page 3 girls.

He bought it mainly for a competition that was in it every week called 'Spot the Ball.' There'd be a photograph of footballers playing a game. The ball wouldn't be in it. You had to put an X where you thought it was. He took great care making his mark each week but he never won. I got caught up in it myself eventually, spending ages trying to work out where the ball was. It was never where you thought. Maybe that was how they made their money.

Another competition he entered was one that was in the 'Sunday Independent.' It was a kind of crossword with multiple choice answers. There'd be a question like 'He did a bad thing and he was…' The answers would be multiple choice ones. You'd be asked to put in words like 'Mad' or 'Bad.'

The crossword was stupid really because the questions made each of the alternatives apply equally to it. Despite that he kept doing it again and again, always without success.

It was the same as with the horses. The only time his ship came in, as he put it, was when we won £1000 on Prize Bonds once. That led to many celebrations, and another cigar coming out like when I revealed the location of the key to his safe when I was a toddler.

Our local GP, Dr McKeever, checked out his health every now and then. He told him he needed to give up whiskey and cigarettes.

He started to drink Guinness now. It wasn't a drink I ever associated with him. Wasn't it the working man's drink? He made the best of it, and of the pipe, but he wasn't happy with either of them.

'What's the point of living forever if you can't enjoy yourself?' he said to me one day, 'You'd be bored to tears.' I knew what he meant. It was like the old joke, 'Staying off bad things doesn't make you live longer. It just seems like it.'

He was never much good at lighting the pipe. Something always seemed to go wrong. He'd use about a half a box of matches trying to get it going.

Each time he was finished with one he'd throw it into the grate. Often he missed and it caught the bedspread. He'd ring the bell for my mother to come in and douse the flame. It became such a regular occurrence we didn't get worked up about it.

It was like, 'Dad set the bed on fire again today. No big deal.'

Bonding

One night when there wasn't much happening I brought him to the pictures with me. He wouldn't have been seen dead at most of the films I went to but he agreed to come to one called 'The Vanishing Point.' It was a fairly routine thriller but he seemed to enjoy it. When it finished I asked him what he thought of it.

'Not too bad,' he said. That was high praise for him for anything made after 1950.

It was raining as we came out. Ironically, the man who was renowned for carrying umbrellas even on the hottest days didn't have one to keep us dry now. What would Sean Bocht have thought?

We sheltered in the foyer of a hotel a few doors up, one called The Royal Dublin.

'This is a nice place,' he said, 'Have you been here before?' I told him I dropped into it sometimes to have a coffee and maybe write a film review.

'Would you like a drink?' he said then. I was surprised as he hadn't said anything about that before we left the house. I'd been with him in the Addison Lodge, a bar close to us, a few times but never on my own.

'Why not,' I said.

I expected him to go to the counter. I'd always associated him with standing at counters in Ballina. It was where he held forth, commanding audiences, master of all he surveyed. He'd always been at the counter anytime my mother asked me to fetch him from a bar in Ballina when he was late home and she was worried about him. But he didn't go there now. Instead he sat down at a table.

He asked me to get him a glass of Guinness. I ordered a pint of Smithwicks for myself.

It was strange sitting beside him having a drink. I remembered all the times in Ballina where I would be having a mineral beside him and asking him if he'd be coming home soon. Pubs were like alien worlds to me in those days, worlds of strange conversations, meaningless laughter, alien smells. Now things were different. We were on an equal footing. I could talk to him about the ways of the world. We could exchange views. Our two generations were one.

'Don't mind me if you want to write a review,' he said, 'I'll just sit here.' I told him I hadn't gone to it for that reason.

'How is life with you?' he said to me then. It was as if he hadn't seen me in a long time.

In a sense maybe he hadn't. How well does anyone know a person they see every day of their lives but don't connect with except on the level of small talk? Do we really know what's going on in their minds or they in ours? When you peel away all the layers of an onion, what's left?

I rattled on about a few things. As I talked to him I wondered if this was what all other father-son relationships were like, people shooting the breeze about mundanities. We were boringly normal with one another.

He didn't share any outstanding revelations with me that night. In the old days he would have drank faster. Now he just sipped his drink. He had a whiskey chaser after the Guinness. Then he reverted to the person I expected, telling me he felt like an anachronism in the world around him.

'My day is gone,' he said, the familiar mantra. He recycled some old stories about his heyday as if to emphasise the point. They weren't as funny as I expected and he wasn't as animated telling them as he usually was but in a strange way that made them more compelling.

After he was finished he looked at the drinkers who were sitting at the tables around us, observing the kind of people he saw all too seldom from his eyrie in the Villas. The night threw shadows over them, bathing them in the half glow of the optics.

In former times he'd probably have gone over to some of them and introduced himself. Did he miss doing that? Did he miss not telling his stories to them? Maybe he wasn't even thinking these thoughts. Each phase of our lives is right for that time because we're going through it. When we get over them we say, 'How could I have done that?' But when we were doing it, it was the right thing for us.

There was a person sitting opposite us in a dress. They appeared to have a moustache. He looked perplexed.

'Is that a man or a woman?' he said. I said I couldn't tell. He raised his eyes to heaven. I thought of his comment, 'A mannish woman is the worst of men.'

'If that's what the world is coming to,' he said, 'Maybe I should have stayed at home.'

He was quiet after that. I wasn't sure why. Maybe it was because he didn't have an audience. There were only a few people in the hotel because of the bad weather.

He watched them coming and going through the revolving doors, making a few comments on the way they were dressed. The person who could have been a man or a woman went out. A few girls came in, laughing and joking together. He watched them mesmerised. 'People are wearing anything and everything nowadays,' he said.

The night ground to a close. I felt flat but in a strange way relieved. Things could have gone worse. I promised myself I'd bring him out again sometime soon. It might have done him some good even if it didn't seem like it. The highs and lows of the past were gone. We were just people now, doing our best to fill in the hours.

After we left the hotel we stood outside at a taxi rank. I probably should have rung for one. There was always a run on them on wet nights.

I asked him if he'd agree to go home on the bus. There was a time he wouldn't have but he did now. It didn't suit him. As we lurched through the streets I wondered if he was thinking of his hackneys, of Pat Hughes, of the days travelling down the country to get documents signed.

'We should do this again,' I said. He said, 'You'd probably prefer someone of your own age.' I told him that wasn't true.

We finally got home. He had trouble walking from the bus, wheezing bronchally for the last stretch. He was too proud to let me link him.

My mother was relieved to see us home. We were gone so long she was concerned that he might be 'tight,' as she put it. 'Was the film any good?' she said. 'I've seen worse,' he said, 'It passed an hour or two.'

He was in reasonably good form over the next few days. Then something happened to change things for him. He got a letter from a man in Ballina to say a woman he used to date had died. He was the executor of her will. Her widower now wanted to buy him out of the executorship.

He told my mother he was thinking of going to Ballina to sort things out. She didn't think that was a good idea. 'Why don't you just give it to him?' she said. He considered doing that for a while but then he changed his mind. 'I don't even want the executorship,' he said, 'but he's so anxious to buy me out of it, it's making me suspicious.'

He travelled to Ballina to contest the matter. I was surprised at his decision. He hadn't been there for years. In fact he hadn't been anywhere for years.

He went down on the train with my mother. The moment he entered the man's house, he said afterwards, he knew something was wrong. A solicitor he had with him was reading a newspaper upside down. It made him suspicious from the word go.

He was always sensitive to details like that. The solicitor was also overly polite to him. 'When people are too nice to you,' he said, 'They're hiding something. You can bet your house on it.'

Heated negotiations went on over the next few days. Different money offers were tossed around to entice him to give up the executorship. He told the man he thought they were too low. Larger ones were also rejected by him. Eventually he decided to walk away from any deal. The man wasn't pleased. He said he was going to take the matter to court.

He rang Dublin the next night. 'Why don't you take the money?' Keith said. He was on my mother's side. He said he didn't want to do that. There was still a fighter in him.

I asked him if he was confident of winning the case. 'That remains to be seen,' he said, 'as the cat said when she came out from behind the wardrobe.' It was good to see he still had fire in his belly.

Because it was a civil case instead of a criminal one, things were put in motion quickly. He was on the phone every night telling us what was happening. On the day of the case, my mother told me, he was like he used to be in his prime, arguing his points with the same energy he had when he first started practicing.

The judge ruled in his favour. The man had to give in. 'He had no case,' my father said, 'He was just crying wolf. I knew that from the word go.' It was a small victory for him but an important one. It made him feel he still represented something.

When he got back to Dublin he was high. He related details of the trip as if he'd won a High Court case. It was great to see him back to his old self. He did his recitations with a new verve. The old jokes were trotted out. We counted the minutes to the well-practised punchlines as we watched him perform.

A few days later I saw him looking at a concert on television. He was entranced, moving his hands like the conductor as if he was in front of the orchestra himself. He seemed to be able to transport himself into these situations, striking an imaginary baton up and down in time to the one on the television. Church music transported him into those kinds of realms sometimes. I used to find myself that way when I listened to Elvis singing gospel songs.

He wasn't drinking much now. I bought him a six pack of Guinness to celebrate. There was a little piece of plastic that came with it. It had a gizmo attached to it that you pumped into the drink to get a head on it. It was strange looking at him with a 'Guinness moustache' as he drank it.

Some nights he joined us for a drink down in the 'Addison.' The proprietor, Mr Freyne, was an old world figure who made him feel important. If he got any kind of feedback at all from someone it put him into good form. Because he wasn't seeing many people in the general run of things, a friendly word from anyone meant more to him than it might have otherwise.

There weren't as many of the family around either, or at least all the time. We'd been dwindling since the turn of the decade. Like Keith, Hugo was married now. Whenever he could he came over to Glasnevin often from Goatstown.

Keith was coming over as much as ever. He talked a lot about films, being more taken with the 'oldies' even than my father ever was. Myself and Hugo, meanwhile, trumped the new ones. My father usually sat on the edge of these conversations. He reminded me of Marlon Brando's Don Corleone as he 'gracefully grew old.'

Keith and myself had always got on well. There was only one night that I remember us falling out. I can't remember what it was about. We actually had a physical fight about it. I'm sure drink was a factor. We were after coming back from the 'Addison' that night. The two of us rolled round the kitchen floor with my father standing above us puffing his pipe and enjoying it no end.

His dark moods continued to oscillate with his childish ones. Malthusian pronouncements would be followed by him going into hysterics at a Charlie Chaplin film or a Laurel and Hardy one.

His mood usually lifted when we brought him into our conversations. We helped him get over his depressions by listening to him. He'd stop talking about the dire state of the world after a certain time. That made me realise it wasn't the world that was the problem for him but the fact that he was outside it.

He'd arrive into the kitchen in his smoking jacket in the middle of the night to corner one of us for a chat. Sometimes he mightn't even have his pyjama top on, just a vest. It was such a difference to the way he was in Ballina. In a strange way that was comforting. It meant he was relaxed.

He made more of an effort if people were in the house in the middle of the day, especially visitors. He'd saunter into the kitchen puffing his pipe. Maybe he'd pour a cup of tea for himself. You'd know he was waiting to be drawn into the conversation.

I wondered what he would have been like with his own father. Would he ever have wandered into a kitchen for a chat with him or any of his family when they were young? Would my mother's father with his? I doubted it. That was what was different between their age and ours.

I couldn't see anything of his father in him apart from his liking for dressing up. They both had the same interest in prestige but my father hadn't the pragmatic sense to follow up on it. One man spent his life in business, the other came into the university generation.

Neither of them had the same intimacy with their parents that my family had in our era. If my father rarely talked about his father, we never stopped talking about him, or writing about him. I'm even doing it now. Would he have written a book about his father? I couldn't imagine it.

Would my mother about hers? That would have been even more unlikely. They came from a different Ireland, one where people kept their feelings to themselves, where the prospect of a long night's journey into day could hardly happen. They didn't glow over their children the same way a later generation would.

Our first steps from the e or our first words weren't captured on Smartphones for all the world to see. In some ways it was a nicer time. People had experiences without making a song and dance about them. They weren't conscious of themselves having these experiences like my generation was, analysing them to the nth degree. If my grandfather had anything to say to my father I expected it to be something matter-of-fact rather than emotional, as was the case with us.

We were both night owls. It started in Ballina where the door was always open. People dropped in for a chat after coming from the Estoria at all hours. I was too young to be a part of these conversations at first but I'd hear the voices from my bed upstairs. In later years I joined them. It was worth it even if my eyes were falling out of my head the next morning.

The teachers at Muredach's gave me a hard time for being 'away with the fairies' on such mornings. It was easier to do your own thing in UCD. Nobody cared if you went to the lectures or not. Maybe my father was the same in Trinity. How many universities turned people into nocturnal animals?

I was easy prey for him at night. 'Am I keeping you up?' he'd say. But I wanted to be. It was different in the daytime. If I was rushing out somewhere I wouldn't be able to indulge him. 'you're like the scarlet pimpernel,' he'd say.

I felt bad about that but we all knew how long his stories went on when he got going on them.

In the absence of any of us he'd make for someone like June's friend Myra from Griffith Avenue, or some of Audrey's friends, or Hugo's.

Marius, our next door neighbour, was inclined to drop in every now and again. He enjoyed her when he was in form for her but he could never guarantee he would be. That was the problem with someone who called without an invitation. If he didn't feel up to talking to her June would whisk her up to the Maples, a pub that was near us.

I don't remember him going to the Maples much, or the Sunnybank, another local. The 'Addison' was classier. If he'd had a drink he got sentimental. He'd complain about the world being cruel, about us needing to be protected from it. Then the next morning everything would be back to normal. God would be in his heaven and all would be right with the world.

Sometimes he talked about his father, how he never really got to know him. Or he'd go on about Trinity, or my mother, how she changed his life, or about Ballina and the ins and outs of his relationships with the other solicitors, the petty rivalries that went on between them.

'Eventually you become the last person you wanted to be,' he said to me one night. Maybe that was inevitable when you lived in a town where you saw the same people day after day and night after night. His world became shrunk into their dimensions. To survive the repetition he adapted himself to its ways.

When he was in form for talking he didn't mind how many people were there but if he wasn't he didn't stand on ceremony. We'd be delegated to say he was asleep. He liked telling a joke Oscar Wilde told about a friend of his who said to him, 'I passed your house last night.' Wilde replied, 'Thank you.'

His jokes got cornier. We pleaded with him not to tell the same ones over and over.

Sometimes he hadn't even remembered that we'd heard them. We cringed at their reiterations but then he'd start laughing and we'd find ourselves laughing along with him. 'It was a good one, wasn't it?' he'd say, 'Dang good.'

A lot of his jokes concerned social status. There was one he told about a man who wanted to marry a girl from a better background to him. 'Before he popped the question,' as my father put it, 'he had to question the pop.' .

He asked the man what he was earning. When he told him the amount, the father nearly had apoplexy. He said, 'That wouldn't keep my daughter in handkerchiefs.' At this the suitor stormed out of the house. At the door he saw his would-be fiancé in tears beside her father. 'Goodbye miss Snotty Nose,' he barked at her.

Another story he liked telling was about a man who married a soprano. She was famous for her voice but wasn't much in the beauty department. On the wedding night he looked at her across the bed and said, 'For Christ's sake sing!'

I often wondered why he was so concerned with class. Was it because PJ Malone had gone from one level of society to another? It meant less to my mother because she was born into it.

People who had wealth in their families for generations didn't seem as concerned about it. The 'nouveau riches' did. We weren't that but we were hardly blue blood either. When my grandfather was growing up he probably knew people who'd had experiences of the Famine. That kind of experience would have marked him. Maybe it marked my father as well.

He didn't like the idea of me dropping my double-barrel name. When I told him I found it to be an encumbrance he said the inevitable, 'Don't go against your background.'

How many times did I have to tell him that meant nothing to me, that I didn't want to live in a castle with a moat and drawbridge? 'If you didn't have it,' he said, 'It would.'

I said that was beside the point. Everyone wanted what they didn't have. It was basic human nature. Some people would crawl across cut glass to get up the social ladder. They craved it because it was out of their reach. The far away hills were green.

Some nights his jokes, like his recitations, fell flat. It was when he was working too much at them, when he was trying to convince himself he felt better than he did.

Merriment was a way of holding on to us, of preventing us from going out on the town. It was like the old slogan, 'Laugh and the world laughs with you. Cry and you cry alone.'

Memories of the court case kept his spirits up for a few months. He re-lived it in his mind by acting it out for us. But at a certain point even the recreation of this fell flat as well. He'd say things like, 'I've talked too much. I'm even boring myself.'

I hated to see him losing his jizz. When he was depressed in the past he could turn it into black humour. That mitigated it. It made fun of it and often it made it go away.

That wasn't the case now. After the elation of the Ballina trip died down he seemed to be in a different place, somewhere he couldn't get out of no matter how hard he tried.

'Why did he ever bother with it?' my mother said. I was inclined to agree.

He started to forget things. Dates in his diary weren't as exact as they used to be. The discipline he'd practised in Ballina when he was working with clients began to desert him. So did his interest in how he looked. Now and then he might have his dressing gown buttoned wrongly.

June with my parents

One day he put his vest on back to front. He often cut himself shaving. You'd see him with bits of toilet paper stuck to his face. Another time when he was shaving I saw him putting his razor into a cup of tea he had beside him by mistake. 'Blast it!' he said. There was a time he would have laughed at something like that. Now it annoyed him.

I sense his concentration diminishing. He'd read different books simultaneously throughout his life. Now he didn't seem to enjoy doing that anymore. I'd see books open on his bed at certain pages and wonder if he'd finish them. He picked books up and discarded them as if they failed to sustain his interest. Was it that the kinds of books being written now weren't of interest to him or was he losing interest in the activity of reading itself? I couldn't say for sure.

'I feel like a second hand person,' he said to me one night. I thought it might be because he'd lost pride in his appearance. I told him he meant more to me in his pyjamas and dressing gown than in his Trinity rig-out. They made him more real.

He started to make dramatic statements about his life. They were along the lines of ones he'd been making for years but now with more drama attached to them. 'I've crossed the Rubicon,' he said to me one night, 'I'm tired of living and scared of dying.' It was a line from 'Ol' Man River.'

He said he didn't know why any of us were born. 'God must be evil,' he said, adding, 'if there *is* a God.' He usually looked at me when he said that, as if I was expected to contribute my own view. Maybe he thought I was affected by all the atheists I was running into in Belfield, or that I'd succumbed to Jean-Paul Sartre's idea of hell as 'other people.'

Religion, he said, was 'Apple pie in the sky when you die.' He wanted to put God in the witness box when he saw him. I tried to imagine the scenario. He'd be saying to God, 'Do you swear, by almighty God, to tell the truth, the whole truth and nothing but the truth?' I was reminded of the old joke, 'What would you say to God if he sneezed? God bless you?'

The conservative in him echoed the views of 'educated' Catholics like Chesterton. He was a devotee of Thomas Aquinas and his 'proofs' of the existence of God. When I brought up people like Sartre and Camus it was like pouring cold water on his views. And yet when he was in his megrims he seemed to take a 180-degree turn away from them.

My mother hovered on the edges of such discussions with cups of tea at the ready. She was hoping such lapses in judgment would pass. It was like Chanticleer and Pertelote from Chaucer's 'Canterbury Tales.' Pertelote tried to dismiss Chanticleer's dark thoughts as nothing more than indigestion. Maybe it was the difference between men and women the world over.

He'd always enjoyed discussions like this throughout his life. Now that he was the age he was they had more of an edge to them.

There are no guide books for old age. He never found it easy. Nobody who likes a good time does. As we get older it becomes harder to do that. Our bodies betray us and maybe our minds too. The people who negotiate it best are those who don't have highs and lows in life, just a general plateau of uniformity. They rise with the lark and go to bed before midnight, usually falling asleep as soon as their head hits the pillow.

My father could never have been that type of person. The older he got, the more he went on about the fact that he was going to die soon. He had to. He was the age for it. As he put it, 'Anno Domini.'

He told me a story about two old men who were at a funeral. When it was over, one of them said to the other, 'Is it worth our while going home?'

He had another one about an old man and his son at a funeral. As they filed out of the graveyard he said to him, 'You may die tomorrow, but I must.' It was black humour but he giggled at it, the monocle popping out as ever when he came to the punchline.

Valediction

In late 1976 Ann Reihill, the widow of our cousin Paddy Dillon-Malone, started a fashion magazine called 'Image.' Paddy was Uncle Louis' son. He was a businessman who wrote a groundbreaking book called 'An Analysis of Marketing.'

They were both at Clive's ordination in 1969. A photograph was taken of them talking to my father. Paddy looked devilishly handsome, like Tyrone Power with curly hair and glasses. Ann looked gorgeous in a hat that waved all over the place. My father was holding forth with them about something as he tended to do, especially at public events. They all looked so happy but Paddy would be in his grave a few short years afterwards.

I told my father once that I wished he'd called me Paddy instead of Aubrey. He said, 'Why? Aubrey is a nice name.'

'It's too flowery,' I said.

The problem with parents choosing their children's names is that they choose them because they like them themselves. They don't usually think about what their children might like.

The fact that he liked to call attention to himself meant he went for extravagant names. He'd probably have liked it if his father called him Aubrey. I'd have liked it if he called me Hugh. I didn't ask him if I was named after Aubrey Bourke or Aubrey De Vere. It didn't matter now.

I told him I'd like to write for 'Image.'

'Under what name?' he said.

I said, 'What do you mean?'

He said, 'I'm pulling your leg.'

I probably deserved that. I said I was using Aubrey for my writing because that was what people knew me as. Otherwise I could change it as many times as I wanted.

He was always very witty. He said he thought I was too. Except he didn't say 'witty,' he said 'quick.'

He used to talk about something called 'l'esprit de l'escalier.' It was a French expression meaning people often thought of clever things to say when it was too late. It would usually be when they were coming down the stairs from a room where the person they were talking to was.

'What appeals to you about 'Image'?' he asked me.

I told him I was interested in somewhere permanent that I could write about films. After I stopped writing for 'TCD Miscellany' I'd been spreading myself then over various broadsheets. It was usually for little or no money. I didn't mind that. Everyone had to start somewhere. I was learning the tricks of the trade. Magazines like 'Hibernia' gave me a chance to review books as well as films.

I told him I needed something to distract me from the prospect of thinking about being a teacher for the rest of my life.

'How do you find so much to say about films?' he said to me. As far as he was concerned you watched it and that was it. There was no need to obsess over it. He was surprised any time he saw me reading a film magazine. In general he didn't think much of the intelligence of stars.

One night we were watching Julie Christie on a talk show. She was being asked what she thought of Los Angeles as a place to live.

'It's very antibiotic,' she said. She meant 'antiseptic.' He was highly amused at her slip of the tongue. 'I rest my case,' he said. I thought he was being a bit hard on her. There were lots of people with less intelligence than Julie Christie in L.A.

A few weeks later he met Ann Reihill in the Shelbourne Hotel for lunch. In the course of it he put my request about doing the column to her.

She agreed to employ me as a film reviewer for the magazine. Thus began a decade-long tenure for me in somewhere I least expected.

'Image' was my first experience of writing to a formula. I was given a deadline and a word count. Both of these were new to me. In the stories I wrote for David Marcus I could write in any style I wanted. The same was true for 'TCD Miscellany.' In 'Image' I discussed genres more than films. Everything fell into a pigeonhole.

The first film I reviewed for Ann was Sidney Lumet's 'Network.' The catchphrase from it was Peter Finch's 'I'm mad as hell and I'm not going to take it anymore.' Sometimes I felt like that too.

My father did as well. He was glad to see me in 'Image.' He hadn't regarded 'TCD Miscellany' as 'real' writing even though it was his alma mater. As for my stories in the 'Irish Press,' I don't think they meant much to him either, except for having my byline. 'Image' was printed on glossy paper and was posh. For him it was 'the real McCoy.' That was a pun. McCoy was Ann Reihill's maiden name. He could have made an even better one if he said 'Reihill McCoy.'

The second film I saw for her was 'The Omen.' It was a horror film starring Gregory Peck and Lee Remick. I went to it on February 11. It was going to be printed in the March issue of the magazine.

He brought me breakfast in bed that morning, arriving into my room in his blue pyjamas with the white cord. A cup of watery tea dangled precariously on a plate. It also contained two slices of over-buttered toast.

He sat by the bed puffing his pipe fast, almost a puff a second the way he did when he was excited. A match went flying through the air as he tried to light it. I wondered if one day he'd set my mattress up in flames like he did his own one.

His legs were crossed. One of his feet hopped up and down the way it used to do in court when he was getting ready to make a speech.

'You're going to a film today, aren't you?' he said. I told him a bit about it. He liked Gregory Peck. We'd all seen 'The Guns of Navarone' and 'The Big Country' in the Estoria.

'Will you be back before the coal comes?' he said. We were having some delivered that day.

'Probably,' I said.

I asked him if there was anything he wanted in town. He mentioned a book on Hitler that had just come out. He was always reading about him. That was hardly surprising. He'd lived through the two World Wars. The second one had even come to Ireland. A Luftwaffe regiment dropped bombs on North Strand in Dublin on May 31, 1941, a year to the day before June was born. 28 people were killed in the blast and 300 homes destroyed. They later apologised, claiming it was an accident but what good was that to the 28 people who lost their lives?

Sometimes he'd say things like, 'I wonder if Hitler is in hell.' He wondered if God forgave people like him. He often talked about the Holocaust, about the genocide in Dachau and Belsen, the castrations and disembowelments.

I went into town later that morning. I bought the book for him and went to the film. It was scary and it unnerved me. Usually these kinds of films didn't. This one was different. I felt a premonition at it.

I went into a café afterwards to write my review. If I didn't do these things immediately I found I lost interest. It was the same with homework at Muredach's. It wasn't that I was a goody-goody. I just couldn't enjoy my evenings if I had something hanging over me to do.

I felt strange on the way home in the bus. Something was wrong but I didn't know what. When I got to the house I felt even stranger.

I turned the key in the door and walked into the kitchen. Everything was quiet. My mother was crying. Audrey was beside her. I felt my throat muscles constricting. When I tried to speak, no words came out.

Finally I managed to say, 'What's wrong?' Nobody replied to me.

I went into my father's room. He wasn't there. The bed was empty. His dressing gown was on top of the Super Ser. I looked out to the back yard. A bag of coal lay scattered on the ground.

I went back out to the kitchen. 'Where is he?' I said. They still didn't speak. It took a few seconds for me to register what was going on.

He was dead.

I sat down on a chair. How could he be? He'd made me my breakfast. We'd talked. He looked as healthy as a trout. He'd never been sick a day in his life.

My mother said, 'He didn't suffer.'

It still wasn't registering with me. Where was he? Was I dreaming?

I came out of my dream. 'What happened?' I said. 'There was an argument,' my mother said.

I took the Hitler book out of my pocket. A clock ticked somewhere. I shook with a weird kind of fear.

'How do you mean?' I said.

The phone rang. It seemed to echo in an empty chamber. I heard a kettle boiling.

Voices were coming from far away, merging into one another. I heard his one in my head.

I saw him coming into my bedroom with the tea and toast, waiting for me to wake up so he could talk to me, watching me wipe the sleep from my eyes.

'There was an argument,' my mother said again. She was still crying. I went over to her. She couldn't talk.

Audrey started to tell me what happened. She said the argument was with the coalman. It was about the amount of bags he'd brought. My father said he'd under-counted. The man got aggressive. My father became worked up.

A moment later he clutched his chest and fell back. Then he lost consciousness.

Had his life become this small that such things mattered? When he was in his prime he wouldn't have noticed if a coalman was twenty bags short, or even thirty. Now he had nothing else to think about but these little events in his day – bringing me breakfast, asking me about the film, waiting for the delivery.

I imagined him being intimidated by the man but not wanting to show it, sticking out his chest as he confronted him, not wanting my mother or Audrey to think he was afraid of him.

In the old says there would have been no need to be. It would have been a case of 'Yes sir, no sir, three bags full, sir.' Now the world had changed. Jack was as good as his master.

I looked at the book about Hitler, a book that would now never be read. For some reason I found myself thinking of the time in Castleknock when the burly rugby player was coming towards him. I imagined him doing his best to stand his ground to prevent him scoring the try he was looking for. The stakes were somewhat different with the coalman. Standing his ground with him didn't just cost him a try. It cost him his life.

Audrey tried to revive him. My mother rang Dr McKeever. Audrey kept working on him but she couldn't get a response from him.

Dr McKeever got to the house within minutes. He started to work on him too but he didn't get anywhere either. After a few minutes he said, 'It's no good. There's nothing I can do. He's gone.'

The ambulance came then. It took him to the Mater. Everyone was going in there later to see him.

The kettle boiled. Audrey gave me a cup of tea. She put her hand around me. I went over to my mother. 'He didn't suffer,' she said again.

We sat in the silence. The clock ticked louder. I looked out at the coal bag in the yard. Was a bag of coal worth a life? There was another one in the glasshouse.

The phone rang again. It was someone from the family, someone from far away, maybe America. I thought of myself watching 'The Omen' some hours before, how scary that title seemed now. I never listened to people when they had premonitions. I never had one before myself. Was this one real?

I went next door again and looked at his things - the tin where he kept his cuttings, his Mick McQuaid tobacco, the burn-stained mattress on his bed, the pipe he struggled to light. I pictured him puffing it, pictured him ringing the bell. He'd never do these tings again.

His diary was beside the bed. I opened it. There was a biro on the spine. Under February 11 he'd written in his familiar squiggle, 'Aubrey went to town. I brought him his breakfast.' I started to cry.

The words of Dr McKeever kept going round in my head: 'It's no good. There's nothing I can do. He's gone.' He would have said them to many people over the years. Another phrase came into my head. It was my father's: 'We kill time and then time kills us.'

I didn't want to see him in the Mater. Was I a coward? Would he have wanted me to? Audrey started talking again but I couldn't hear her. Was she talking to me or to someone on the phone?

Where was he now, I wondered. Was he with God? If there *was* a God. Would he put him in the witness box or would it be the other way round?

He used to talk about whether he was going up or down. 'Most of my friends are downstairs,' he'd say, 'It sounds like more fun.' Heaven for the climate and hell for the company.

He was with Aunt Mary and Lasca and Babette and Dan McGrew and Mido Cooligan and Martin McGrath and Mad Carew in the bourn from which no traveller returned.

I looked over at my mother. She smiled at me through her tears. She wasn't hysterical. I always felt she wouldn't be when this day came. She must have known it would sometime. That didn't make it any easier.

They'd had 'the two days.' He'd been a burden to her all her life but she loved him so she didn't think of it that way. She'd probably have been bored if she was married to someone practical like Uncle Louis. Now she wouldn't have to worry about him anymore. Her 'tenth child' had given up the ghost.

When I woke up the next morning I didn't remember what happened for a few seconds. Then it registered.

I dressed myself in a daze. When I went down to the kitchen my mother was just sitting there. She didn't say anything. I put my arm around her. She put on a cup of tea, the cup of tea that accompanied all tragedies, all trivialities, all everythings, the bottomless cup that travelled from the range in Ballina to the Aga in Glasnevin and was still doing its job of healing. It was one of the few constants from the past. Pour a cup and we'd be all right, we'd be the same people we always were.

As we drank it she talked about who phoned, who was coming home, what time she was going to the hospital. We didn't talk about my father. What would have been the point?

I sat in his room looking at his tin filled with his war chest of cuttings. I didn't open it. It sat there like a tribute to him, the equivalent of his Iona Villas safe, like a jewellery box might be to a woman. It was his go-to place when other things weren't happening. Other things hadn't been happening for a long time now.

I pictured its contents: the family tree clippings, the ones from newspapers with strange events that intrigued him, his records of anything that happened to his flock of nine, the letters from us to him, whether MT or not.

Aftermath

The next few days are jumbled in my mind. Somehow I got through them. I said the kinds of things you're expected to say to people at times like this, the comfortable cliches that pass for conversations when someone close to you dies. They go through their motions and you go through yours. You think one thing and say another and then they go home and it's all right again, at least for a while.

I was furious with the coalman, a man I'd never seen and didn't know anything about. He'd caused the death of my father and nothing was going to be done about it. Did he even know what he'd done?

What if it had been one of us? My father would have been thinking about an action after two minutes. Deezer had bitten a girl under the eye and had to be put down and yet a man had caused the death of another man and still got to go to work the following day without any questions being asked of him. Was that justice?

My mother said, 'Don't blame him. He didn't know what he was doing.' She knew how impetuous my father was, how likely he was to jump to a conclusion.

In her world you didn't do that. You sucked up the pain. It was what got her through all the years with him. She didn't see anyone being at fault. I did, being more like 'Red Hugh.'

Mary came over. She'd been down in Galway with her parents when he died. Her uncle Bernie died that year too. They'd gone down to Glenamaddy for the funeral.

Her father saw the notice about my father in the paper. It was a few hours before he told her. He knew how close she was to him, how upset she'd be. He himself would also die before the year was out.

'I hope he's at peace,' my mother said, 'Hugh had such confusion in his life.' It was strange to hear her calling him by his name. Sometimes she referred to him as 'Daddy.' The only other time I heard that was from the wife of Big Daddy in Tennessee Williams' play 'Cat on a Hot Tin Roof.'

When I dreamt of him he wasn't Happy Dad, he was Confused Dad, floundering around his room in some tizzy over lost files, about money, about displacement. Awake, I tried to think of him when he was at his best, when he was free of his demons, giving us a world we'd never have known without him even if he felt that world turned against him finally. He was larger than life and now he'd lost his one.

I told myself I had to get on with mine without him. He'd got on with his after his own father died. Everyone did. I'd had him longer than many sons had their fathers.

My mother grieved quietly. I felt she'd get by in time too. She'd have our memories of him just like he had his ones to tide him by when he was down. He'd had a long enough life and got out of it quickly.

Dr McKeever said he was an accident waiting to happen. How fortunate he was that he didn't know that. He wouldn't have been able to deal with hospitals, tests, operations.

There was no funeral. He wouldn't be entering the family vault at Leigue. Instead he donated his body to science.

It went to the medical department of Trinity. There seemed to be a kind of logic to it. 'Come in and see me,' he used to say for a joke.

'He was in his seventies, wasn't he?' a neighbour said to me, 'He had a good innings.' I never knew what that expression meant. What did it matter if he was 72 or 22? He was my father and he was gone. That was all I could think of. People felt they had to say something to console you but what they said usually only made you feel worse.

I drank to his memory, hoping he'd be having the party of all parties wherever he was. I hoped he'd be at peace with himself after all the years of tension. Maybe he'd even make up with Aunt Nellie and Aunt Florence and Aunt Eileen. Or would he drive them to 'the other place'? We joked about that as we joked about everything else to do with him, laughing through our tears.

Ann Reihill rang to sympathise. She'd always admired him. If she hadn't, I probably wouldn't have got a job writing for her. She said I didn't have to send in a review that month if I didn't feel up to it. I told her I'd written it before he died. It seemed crazy to be talking about a review in view of what happened but sometimes these things are the only things you can talk about.

We all gathered together in the house remembering him over the following nights. We told his jokes and his stories. Some of us tried to do his recitations but they fell flat.

After we'd done all our grieving we looked to our mother. We felt she wouldn't crumble. In a way that was harder to deal with than if she did. How could you get someone to cry on your shoulder when you'd spent your life crying on her one? Who did Pagliacci go to when he had a problem?

Members of the family who weren't living in Ireland phoned. They mainly spoke to her.

She didn't say much, just that she was doing all right. After she passed the phone to me they'd ask me quietly if that was true. I'd say I didn't know. She didn't talk much to me either. Everyone knew she was the stronger person in the marriage but how could you be strong when something like a death happened?

'You're my job now,' she said to me one day. I thought it was an unusual thing to say. It was as if her life was a sacrifice for others, that such a sacrifice would continue with me.

I said, 'You have to have a life of your own outside me. Otherwise I'd be using you.' She said, 'I don't see it like that. People use chairs for sitting on, don't they? Isn't it good that they're there to be used?'

I didn't know what to say to that. She was going to be a chair and I was going to be sitting on it. I'd get priority over her other children because I was living with her. The ones who went away would get catered for too, of course. They might have left home but they hadn't really. They had 'travelled bodies and untravelled minds.'

They were still with her in their hearts despite being married to other people. They'd continue to return to her year in year out like the swallows that came back to Capistrano in the Pat Boone song. It was almost as if the price of gaining her love was that we ceded our lives to her irrevocably.

'You made me love you,' Keith used to sing to her. He'd go down on one knee to her and sing 'Mammy' in Al Jolson's voice, throwing his arms out like Jolson.

She got through her days somehow and I got through mine. She lay on in bed once or twice in the mornings, something that was unusual for her.

In the kitchen she'd mooch around in her dressing gown like my father used to do. That was unusual too. I searched her face for clues as to how she was feeling but she never gave anything away, passing off all my questions as she always did by changing the subject. How could her life matter when ours were going on?

She still refused to cook a meal for herself. I worried about her appetite. She wasn't even picking at my scraps now.

I listened to her telling people that she was good but I could see the sadness in her. It was in her eyes, in her quietness, in the slow way she moved around rooms, dragging her feet in her slippers.

She didn't talk about my father. She didn't need to. He was the man who brought her out of herself, who gave her nine children. How could life ever be the same again?

I thought of them on the boat on their first date with Aunt Valerie, the way he would have been swaying from side to side of it as the waves lashed against it.

I imagined him thinking she wanted a macho man, someone to protect her from such wild waves, and her being amused by him, just wanting him to like her, macho or not, and laughing with that big laugh of hers as she threw her head back.

She hadn't a care in the world then, this country girl who only wanted to dance her way around Roscommon in those days, Patsy Conry, the calmest of all the family before life got to her like it got to all of us.

Over the next few weeks I found myself going into rooms looking through all his papers, those dusty old files that smelt of him, making a jigsaw of his past the same way he used to as he traded in one life for another. Whenever I went into his bedroom I expected to see him smoking his pipe in that fast motion he had, or pulling some article from a newspaper to show me. No longer would he write letters to them denouncing the sate of the modern world. It would have to wend its way to destruction without him.

I took out copies of his letters to the 'Irish Times,' to the 'Western People,' to anywhere else he sent his ramblings after the world stopped making sense to him, after he assumed a new identity, a kind of Malthusian one, warning everyone about the Armageddon ahead and then tearing the bottom out of it with his wit.

Afterwards I looked at all my own papers. On the surface they couldn't have been more different from his ones. We were from different eras but the same addiction to clutter was at work, the same inability to throw anything out. I found poems of mine that went back to the Ballina days, pieces of doggerel like he used to write, scattered speculations on anything and everything. They didn't matter anymore but I still couldn't part with them.

I started tidying everything. Freudians would probably have said I was trying to impose some order on my life now that the centre of it was gone. I was starting afresh, becoming reborn into a new world to replace the old one as I did when I left Ballina, when I left anything in my life, or when anything left me, sloughing off a skin, putting on that metaphorical new set of clothes, reinventing myself for a new era.

Or maybe I was just trying to keep myself busy.

Loss

Losing a father is like losing a limb. I can't say I felt the sense of a protective covering being taken away because at the end of his life I felt I was minding him as much as he was minding me. But he was still my father, with all that entailed.

I thought of the times when he was like a character from a Charles Dickens novel to me, of the days when he was silly, of the days when his moods fluctuated like the weather.

My friend was gone. There would be no more late night chats, no more childish sniggering, no more sights of his body shaking with laughter over the jokes I used to complain about and now missed.

I thought of the red velvet cushion he used to get from me at the Estoria, the way he'd chat with Paddy Mulligan until the lights went down and the picture was about to start, the crackle I'd hear on the celluloid as the names of the cast came down before the magic began.

I still continued to go out at night. It made me feel guilty leaving my mother but I did it. I knew she'd have wanted me to stay in even if she didn't say it. She never had to. It wasn't her style to cramp anyone's else's one. She just gave that big smile of hers and said, 'Go out and have a good time for yourself.'

She made me feel guilty. It would have been easier for me if she was a selfish person, if she was someone who held on to me against my wishes. Then I wouldn't have been beating myself up in the bars or the cinemas or the snooker halls or wherever I was. How sharper than a serpent's tooth it was to have a thankless child.

On the odd night I stayed in she told me stories about her early days with my father, of how he took her out of herself every time they went to a function. 'He only had to enter a room to make me feel at home in it,' she said.

When he died I told myself that if I had him back even for a day I'd give myself over to listening to these stories. I had a chance to do that with my mother but I didn't take it. We rarely learn from our mistakes in life. We just repeat them.

We got back to our routines. She did her work and I did mine. We had nights where we reminisced and nights where we did nothing.

The family called whenever they could. If they had a problem they asked her about it. She always seemed to be able to solve these problems with her insights, insights that didn't seem to need to be worked at, that just shot out of her without effort.

When they were going away she'd be sad. Sometimes she'd cry. If she did I'd think of my father's words, 'In every parting there's the image of death.' Maybe that was why he got so emotional at Dublin Airport that time when Audrey was going away to Surrey to be a nurse.

Life moved on. We talked about other things: films, work, television. We had to. There was no point worrying the wound.

1977 eventually came to an end. It was a year I was relieved to see the back of, a year where I lost a man I never really knew despite thinking I did.

I was 23, the same year he was when he lost his own father. I wondered how that death affected him. He rarely talked about it. He hadn't been close to his father when he was growing up. He idolised him but idolatry wasn't love. It was an idolatry tinged with fear. They were too different. He was always conscious of his father's disapproval of how he was living his life.

When he died he started to feel sad about him. That always happens when someone dies. The threatening aspect of them goes away. I felt it when I heard of the death of teachers in Muredach's who used to put fear in me. They're dead so they can't do anything to us anymore. They can't stop us spending money and they can't give out to us about not studying or going to the pictures or getting our homework wrong. We start to feel sorry for them then. We regret the times you could have spent trying to get to know them instead of being afraid of them. Unfortunately, it's too late then. At this stage we start to feel sorry for ourselves as much as them.

My grandfather's death coincided with the beginning of my father's seriousness, a seriousness you can see in the photographs of him taken at this time of his life more than any other. It brought death to the forefront of his life and made him start thinking of the big questions – where we came from and where we're going.

PJ Malone died saying the rosary.

Recovery

I went back to Pat's eventually. My mother encouraged me to. If she was the one who died there was no way he'd have done that. It would have been like the situation in Ballina where he was easier to get around when I wanted to get off school.

'You need to get back into something,' she said.

I knew she was right but I didn't want to. If I hadn't much interest in my studies before he died I had even less now. Doing essays was out of the question.

The last thing I wanted to be was a teacher. As the saying went, there was no chalk in my blood. Hugo was cut out for teaching because he was a performer. In that he was like my father. I wasn't.

One of my classmates asked me why I hadn't been attending lectures recently. I said, 'My father died.'

His mouth hung open. What can you say when someone tells you something like that?

He tried his best to be normal with me but it was hard talking about other things afterwards. A month before we'd been joking about lecturers. Now we wouldn't be able to joke about anything.

I thought a trip back to Ballina might help me. I applied for teaching practice in my old alma mater on the Killala Road across from Aunt Nellie's house. I was accepted but then the weather got cold and the roads became impassable. I ended up not being able to go down. It was as if someone was conspiring against me.

I tried to study but the words of books kept swimming in front of me. My mother said I should go up to Dr McKeever. She thought he might be able to prescribe something for me. By 'something' I presumed she meant a bottle of the famous Valium.

I went up to him a few days later. I sat in the waiting-room in a chair beside a table that reminded me of our mahogany one in Ballina. His son was crawling in and out under it the way I used to do when I was his age. He had a patch over one of his eyes.

Dr McKeever came out.

'Lazy eye,' he said, 'I put the patch over the strong one to make the other one work harder.' I thought of my father and his monocle.

'Good idea,' I said.

He asked me how I'd been since my father died.

'Up and down,' I said.

I wondered how many of his other patients would have passed away since my father. Ten? Twenty? Death would have been part of his daily routine. Maybe doctors reached a point of immunity with it all.

'What can I do for you?' he said.

'I'm finding it difficult to concentrate,' I said.

He wrote something on a piece of paper.

'Take one a day,' he said, 'They'll cool you down.' I presumed they were Valium. I didn't refuse them. My mother had been giving me so many since my father died she must have been close to being out of them.

He started to talk about my father.

'He had so many stories,' he said, 'I always liked hearing them. He really acted them out. The last thing he wanted to talk about was his health.'

He looked at me as if I was expected to say something but I couldn't think of anything. Then he said, 'He lived in a very narrow orbit, didn't he?'

I didn't know what he meant. Was it an accusation?

'He was a recluse,' I said. I didn't want to make it sound like an apology. Recluses were my favourite kind of people. All the great inventions were made by recluses, weren't they? Weren't all the great books written by them? I felt depressed going home that day. I felt he'd disrespected his memory.

I graduated from Pat's that summer. Then began the hard part – looking for a job. I did the usual rounds, filling in forms and making phone calls to schools. A part of me was hoping they'd say no to me. I thought I'd prefer to be an unemployed teacher than an employed one.

How could I face forty children and act like I knew what I was talking about?

I thought of the old joke about the person who says he's not able to go to school when his mother wakes him one morning. 'I can't,' he says, 'I'm afraid.' She says, 'You have to. You're the teacher.'

A lot of other people died that year besides my father and Mary's: Maria Callas, Joan Crawford, Peter Finch, Bing Crosby, Charlie Chaplin, Groucho Marx. He loved Charlie Chaplin. I preferred Groucho.

Elvis Presley died in August. He was only 42. I knew he wasn't well from articles I'd been reading about him in newspapers in recent years. They always used euphemisms like, 'Mr Presley has been hospitalised due to exhaustion.' Anyone who knew anything about him knew it was much more than that. The little articles in the papers about his kidney problems or his twisted colon didn't mention that he was taking the kind of medication terminal cancer suffers were prescribed by doctors to get himself up for his stage performances.

It was Keith who gave me the news. He was on his way out to work at the time. I was in bed. He stuck his head in the door of the bedroom and said, 'Elvis died.'

I was half asleep as he spoke those words. I fell back into that sleep after he spoke them. When I woke up I wasn't sure if I'd been dreaming. It was like the morning I woke up after my father died, when I wasn't sure what happened for a few seconds. Had Keith really put his head in the door? Had he really said what he said? It was only when I turned on the radio that I knew it was true.

Elvis was gone like my father was. They died within six months of one another. They both died of coronaries, one caused by a coalman, the other by the fear of reaction to a kiss-and-tell book written by his bodyguards that had just been published. These things, of course, were just catalysts. Neither man had taken care of their health. Both of them were larger than life and now both had lost those lives.

They'd both been closer to their mother than their father growing up. Both were shy and both were performers. Both sucked the oxygen out of a room when they entered it. Both had addictive personalities. Both were also night owls. Like my father, he liked reading through the night, and would wake his wife up to tell her if he found something interesting in a book. He also spoiled his daughter more than his wife did. If she wanted to get off school, no more than ourselves, it was to him she'd go rather than her mother.

I thought back to the days in Ballina listening to Elvis on Radio Luxembourg, his voice seeming to come from a crypt as he sang 'Are You Lonesome Tonight.' I loved the way he spoke the words in the middle of it: 'Honey you lied when you said you loved me, and I had no cause to doubt you. But I'd rather go on hearing your lies than go on living without you.'

I went into Easons later that day. I bought every newspaper I could see. They had him all over the front pages as if he was a head of state. To me it was more like a member of the family who'd died.

Marc Bolan died the same week but nobody seemed to notice. Two people were killed at Elvis' funeral in Graceland but nobody seemed to notice that either. The king was dead, long live the king.

I wrote a tribute to him the following week It was printed in the 'Western.' The editor, Terry Reilly, gave me a full page. I'm sure my father would like to have seen it. I'd never had a full page in any newspaper before. Maybe it would have made up for Sean Bocht.

June got married later that week. Donie O'Donoghue came to the wedding. At one stage he jumped up on the wedding table and started doing Elvis impressions. Then Hugo did.

Basil got married later that month. Audrey got married around that time as well. It was as if my father's death left the family sundered. We all needed new nests. The figurehead was gone. I thought of cowboy films where the Indians retreated when the chief was shot.

People often asked me where I was when Elvis died. It felt boring telling them I was in bed at the time. It was even more boring telling them where I was when John F Kennedy was shot. I was on the floor of the dining room at the time, watching a television programme with Peter Lawford – who I learned afterwards was related to him.

The month after June's wedding I got a job in a small school outside Blanchardstown. At the interview the principal told me I was second preference to a man they'd interviewed earlier that day. The news didn't do much for my confidence. He told me I'd be starting the following week.

'Don't smile before Christmas,' he advised.

I knew I'd be nervous walking into the classroom for the first time. I took out Dr McKeever's bottle of Valium and looked at it. Written on the side were the words, 'Keep Away From Children.'

In the end I went into the classroom cold turkey on the first day. Like my father in the courthouse, maybe I needed the adrenalin. I got on better with the pupils than I expected. They were a mixture of boys and girls. That would have been unthinkable when I was growing up in Ballina. Having a girl in my class in Muredach's would have been like having a Martian in it – or a Protestant.

My favourite pupils were the ones who weren't bright, the ones who had no interest in school. They reminded me of myself in Muredach's. People said to me, 'If you hate school that much, why did you become a teacher?' I could never answer that question. 'Masochism,' was all I could offer by way of an explanation.

I lost myself in the job over the next few months. Work always did that, at least up to a point. I wasn't a conventional teacher. The fact that I was the youngest of a family meant I knew little about children. They were a novelty to me so I spoiled them. I was meant to be 'in loco parentis' but I was hardly that. Maybe 'loco' period would have been a better description.

It was a country school. Mice ran across the floor some days, scaring the life out of everyone. Birds flew into the cloakroom. The children had unusual names and unusual accents. I got to know some of their parents as well as themselves. It was a closely-knit community. I felt part of something.

Hugo told me I should go in for secondary teaching. I tossed around the idea of doing the H. Dip, putting it on the long finger. For now it was being in 'loco parentis,' as they said. In secondary you taught subjects, in primary you taught children. Or so they said.

I tried to think of new ways to do the job every day. I wondered how I could sell an idea to them, or a language, or a mathematical equation.

After a while it wasn't an act anymore. It was real. They started to respond. At a certain time I convinced myself that maybe I could make a go of this life. Maybe I could be a junior Hugo, another pedagogue ministering to younger minds, developing them in a way that had never been done to mine in Muredach's.

I talked to my father after he died. Whenever I had to do something difficult I asked him for his advice. It might have been when I had to face a classroom of children or some other situation. I thought of him in similar circumstances in front of a judge or a policeman during a difficult case. I identified with his nerves. Sometimes my mother popped a Valium into my mouth at times like this just like she did to him.

One night I said to her, 'Maybe I can renew my faith in the educational process by being at the front of it.' So many teachers of my youth seemed to take delight in finding out what we didn't know rather than what we did to give them a right to beat us.

I tried not to think too much about my father. I advised her to do the same. Neither of us were sure that was possible but we tried. The wound was still raw. It was more raw for her than me but she didn't say that. We leant on one another in all the nights following, the blind leading the blind into an empty ditch.

Memories

My father entered into a fond place in my head over the next few years. Anyone I met who knew him talked about the way he dressed, his imposing airs, his ability to captivate people with a yarn. They'd go on at length about him and then, almost by way of an afterthought, add, 'Your mother is a saint.' It was as if there was nothing you could say about her but that. He got the attention and she got the awe.

I told myself he'd had a good life. He didn't have much to look forward to at the time he died. From that point of view it wasn't a tragedy.

Bad memories sometimes got in the way of good ones. I thought of the times when he was worried, when his problems tumbled down on him so much he seemed helpless under them. Then I remembered him when he came out of these times, when he was in charge of his life, or as much in charge of it as any of us can be.

He personified the past to me, a past that bundled uneasily into the present. I gave out to him about his immersion in it but at a certain point of time I fell into that pit too.

They say we spend the first half of our lives rebelling against our fathers and our second half turning into them. I never rebelled against my one but as the years went on I found myself turning into him. I thought of the quote of Mark Twain, 'When I was a boy of 14 my father was so ignorant I could hardly stand to have the old man around, but when I got to 21 I was astonished at how much he'd learned.'

I bought books by the authors he read and stopped reading the ones I'd tried to get him in on. I watched films from the thirties and forties, the ones he would have seen in the Estoria before I was born, ordering them from a dealer in Canada who specialised in old films.

Many of them were grainy. They had crackles on the soundtracks but in a way that made them more authentic. I imagined him watching them in the Estoria with my mother, winding down after a day in Bridge Street, becoming immersed in a world of dinner jackets and dress dances. There was also the other aspect of them, the speakeasies and Prohibition rackets.

Anytime I saw a film with 'Edward Robinson' in it I thought of him in his white scarf. Whenever I saw Charles Coburn I thought of him wearing his monocle. When I saw films with Ramon Novarro and Ivor Novello I thought of him too. He often spoke of these two actors in the same breath, making me think they had more in common with one another than their similar-sounding names.

In 1979 I went on a fly-drive holiday with some friends from the college where I trained to be a teacher. We crossed a border every other day as we made our way from Barcelona to Athens. One of the people on the trip said he wanted to cross as many borders as possible to have more stamps on his passport than anyone he knew. Seeing the countries didn't seem to matter to him, just getting the stamps. He was like a precursor of our modern age where the exposition of images on a Cameraphone seemed to do away with the need for experience. Maybe Descartes' 'I think therefore I am' needed to be changed to 'I can photograph something therefore it exists.'

I remembered my father's phrase about travelled bodies and untravelled minds. Were we any better than him going through his tin box of clippings, or my mother standing in front of a washing machine watching clothes whirring around? What was the difference between a sunset in Crete or one in Crossmolina?

I thought of our Geography teacher in Muredach's. He had an electric globe that he brought into class sometimes. It lit up when you plugged it in. He used to get excited talking about all the countries on it. The more he talked, the more I became excited too. I made myself believe I'd visit such countries one day. Now that I was doing it, the excitement fell away. They seemed more exciting on the globe.

I stayed at the teaching job even though it was a grind. A lot of it was done on auto pilot. I tried to get some kind of a writing career going in the evenings. There were stories, an attempt at a novel, a lot of purple prose. I didn't spend as much time with my mother as I should have. She said she didn't mind that but it was still selfish of me.

Sometimes we watched films together. The video boom arrived in the eighties. I scoured Xtravision for the old movies my father and Keith loved, turning the house into a little cinema as I put one on after the other, cleaning the heads of the machine out with vodka dipped in an old vest I kept just for that purpose.

I couldn't imagine my father having anything to do with the repeated watching of films on a small screen. Just like he didn't enjoy drinking at home, he wouldn't have liked home movies either. Cinemas, like bars or the church, had the exoticness he craved, the size and the atmosphere and the losing of yourself in all that ritual. Small-sized films, like the side altar in the cathedral, wouldn't have been for him.

Every summer I went as far away from Ireland as I could. In the university years it was to search for excitement. Now it was to recharge my batteries for the slog of school in the autumn.

She phoned me as much as she could whenever I was in America. In 1980 I went to Denver. I was working for a carpenter there.

One day he came in to me from his workshop. He said, 'Another letter from Mrs Malone.'

There had been a few before this. He couldn't understand how a man of my age could be that close to his mother. I was 27. I told him we didn't usually cut the umbilical cord in Ireland until we were in our forties. 'It sounds like a nice country,' he said, screwing up his eyes.

I started to read the letter. There was a lot of news, some of it about the tennis at Wimbledon, or 'Wembledon' as she called it, mixing it up with Wembley.

It was a classic match.

'Now that's what I call tennis,' she wrote.

John McEnroe had beaten Bjorn Borg in the final, thereby ending Borg's five year winning streak. Hugo was glad, she said, but June and Audrey had been up for Borg. She wasn't sure who she was up for. Maybe it was good that there was a new champion.

June and her daughter, Joy, were over with her a lot, she wrote. The three of them spent a lot of time in the park down on the Drumcondra Road.

She watched television, losing herself in the trivia of soap operas. 'Dallas' was the show everyone was talking about, the machinations of JR Ewing. She got hooked on it. Maybe my father would have too if he was alive. Or maybe he'd have hated it. Or got hooked on it and pretended to hate it, like he did with 'Coronation Street.'

Audrey had given birth to her first child. Jacqueline and Keith had their third one. The new generation was replacing the old one, making her feel she could be as relevant as a grandmother as she'd been as a mother and wife.

I flew to London the following summer to see Bob Dylan in the Earl's Court Stadium. It was my first time seeing him live. He blew me away with his power. I thought everyone would be talking about him but they weren't. The big thing in all the newspapers that week was the wedding of Prince

Charles to Diana Spencer. You couldn't pass by a shop window without seeing them in it.

I made an effort to make a go of the teaching when I got back but it was no good. I felt drained every evening. Writing picked me up but I knew I couldn't keep straddling the two things. It wasn't fair to the pupils and it wasn't fair to myself.

I stayed home in the summer of 1982. Sport became an escape from my worries. It was the year of comebacks. Jimmy Connors came out of the wilderness to win Wimbledon after an eight year drought. Alex Higgins won the world snooker championship. In football Offaly ended Kerry's dreams of five All-Irelands in a row by a freak goal from Seamus Darby in the dying seconds of the game.

When the school term began again I found myself dreading facing the children. My energy levels were dwindling but theirs stayed the same.

I started to drink more. 'You're spending too much of your money in the bars,' my mother said. She advised me to buy a house. She thought it would give me some discipline. I had about a tenner in the bank at the time.

The pragmatic side of her that was developed during the marriage with my father came to my rescue. Her widow's mite savings ballooned into what was asked for as a deposit. Within days a mortgage was approved.

I went looking for a house. Sean McDonnell picked one out for me in Stoneybatter in a place called Viking Road. It was like going shopping for a coat or a pair of shoes.

'Yes, I'll take that one please.'

'No problem, sir. Would you like it wrapped?'

It was tiny. I wondered what my father would have said if he saw it. Probably that you couldn't swing a cat in it. But maybe his own father's first house was that size too. I remembered his comment about how my grandfather made his fortune from knowing when to buy and when to sell.

Maybe I could sell my house one day too and make a profit on it.

Having a mortgage cut into my salary. It made me feel it wasn't my own anymore. Making the repayments to the bank every month made me feel as if I was singing for my supper.

The years went on. I found myself falling into a rut but there was nothing I could do about it. Or was there?

Sometimes I told my mother I was thinking of leaving the job. 'That wouldn't be wise,' she'd say, 'especially with the mortgage hanging over you.'

She was right about it imposing a discipline on me. Maybe that was good. It meant I sat in with her more. She said, 'You seem more stable.' I wasn't sure if I was or not. Maybe it was just my circumstances that were making it look like that.

One night she told me she was thinking of going into a convent.

'Why?' I said.

She said, 'It would be something good to do.' I tried to read her mind. Was she thinking that I was 'sorted' now? It was as if she decided to devote herself to the heavenly world now that she wasn't needed on the earthly one anymore? Just as my father thought he could die once his youngest child was set up in a job, she seemed to be doing the same thing now that I was, as she put it, 'stable.'

'What about the family?' I said. She said, 'It was just a thought. I probably won't do it.'

More grandchildren arrived. She became as much a magnet to them as she'd been to us. The swallows and their progeny still returned to Capistrano. She dropped the idea of the convent. It was all about being needed.

She got cancer in 1985. She took the news as casually as she had when she got it in 1969 but I had a bad feeling about it from the outset. I went into denial about it. That was the only way I could deal with it.

After she was taken to hospital I found letters about doctor's appointments that she neglected. It was always the way with her, going back to 1969 when she postponed her mastectomy. You couldn't get away with that forever.

We didn't know how bad she was until the day she was supposed to have had her operation for it. The operation never took place. The tumour was too big.

She died that July. Again I went into denial. Everyone in the family was as devastated as we had been about my father's death. Hers was more drawn out but none the less shocking for that.

Did the cancer come from all those early years she spent smoking? Nobody could tell any more than we could say how my father escaped it. He'd always been afraid of getting 'the bug,' as he called it. If she died before him, he said, he'd have drunk himself to death. He wouldn't have been able to cope without her and we wouldn't have been able to cope with him. At least we were spared that.

I thought of the opening lines of Albert Camus' 'The Outsider,' the book that meant so much to Hugo and later to me: 'Mother died today. Or maybe it was yesterday. I don't know.' Such words chilled me to the bone when I first read them. They resonated even more now. Like Meursault, I felt I couldn't feel for her. I didn't allow myself to because I felt too much.

I didn't go to her funeral. As Arthur Miller said when Marilyn Monroe died, 'What would have been the point? She wouldn't be there.' Instead I went down to Dollymount Beach. I looked out to sea as seagulls squawked around the sky.

At one stage a fox trotted by me. The lights of the Pigeon House flicked on and off. The moon was hiding behind a cloud. I thought of the night Neil Armstrong stepped on it, when I watched him doing that on my last night in the house in Ballina, when I ran out and compared it to the moon in the sky.

I wondered where she was. She never liked anyone thinking about her. Maybe we'd start now.

Someone said to me earlier in the day, 'She's gone straight up.' It was nice to have that faith, the penny catechism faith that carried her through all her trials, even a tinge of depression she'd suffered in her last years. 'She's with your father,' Someone else said. I found myself saying, 'I hope he's not keeping her awake tearing out articles from newspapers.'

Her death hit me harder than his. It was lingering. I wasn't ready for it. He'd had a painless escape from life but she didn't. Why was the saint punished and the 'sinner,' as he often described himself, got out quickly. It didn't make sense.

Grief sometimes sits inside you like a lump. If you have enough of it you develop a second skin to cover it. It doesn't take it away but it hides it from other people. Either that or you go into denial. When you do that you don't think people notice. You're like a child hiding in a wardrobe during a game of Hide and Seek, thinking that when you cover your eyes nobody can see you.

I put my hands over my eyes for a long time when my mother died. When I came out of it, I didn't expect anyone to say 'How are you now?' and they didn't.

Instead they talked about how the cancer happened, about how it never should have. If she got it some years later maybe she could have been saved. 'Every age has its disease,' she used to say, 'Then we cure it and a different one comes along.'

It was her simple folk wisdom, the language of Patsy Conry, the country girl from Raheen plonked into an alien world where her dreams of dancing her way around Ireland became transmuted into being Mother Courage.

Children tend to beat themselves up for not spending more time with their parents after they die. I didn't do that with my father but I did with my mother. With him there was some excuse. A lot of things were happening in my life. With her I was just out because I was out. That gnawed at me afterwards. She was too much of a magnet for people to ever suffer from the empty nest syndrome but she deserved more from me.

After one parent dies, the other is left. When a second one does, you feel like an orphan. That's despite whatever age you are. The actor Clifton Webb was very close to his mother. When she died at the age of 91 in 1960 he'd just turned seventy.

Noel Coward said, 'It must be terrible to be orphaned at 71.' He wasn't joking. I felt a bit like that.

Members of the family came home from overseas for her funeral. It was the last time we were all together. A photograph was taken of us in the front garden of the Villas. The last time we were all photographed together was in 1955. It was before Keith and Clive left Ballina.

We were like steps of a stairs then in descending order of height. Now we just stood in a ring. The difference in our heights was hardly noticeable. Also different was the expressions on our faces. In 1955 we'd all been smiling. Now none of us were. We were older if not wiser, carrying the battle scars of a life she'd just left.

The reunion of us all was like a testament to her status. It hadn't happened when my father died. The matriarch was gone now, the one who pulled the strings, the 'real' head of the house. 'The father is the head but the mother is the neck and the neck turns the head.' She was the one who kept the ship afloat when he couldn't. She was the stillness behind him as he performed.

It was strange for us all being together again. Ruth even made the trip from New Jersey. That was something that surprised us all. She hadn't been home since she got married in the seventies. I felt there was little chance she'd change on that decision.

She always said it would be too painful for her to come home because of the thought of going back. It was a bit like me saying to my father that I hadn't wanted to go home to Ballina on visits after we came to Dublin first because of the fear of the same kind of nostalgia. If you didn't think of a place, the sadness for it was that much less. I thought of myself in comparison to her, in comparison to all my brothers and sisters.

In some ways I felt like the Prodigal Son. It was the opposite of the Bible story where the Prodigal was the one who went away. My mother killed the fatted calf for me on many occasions, and cooked it as well. Now I'd have to cook my own ones, if I bothered.

The house felt empty after she died. Keith sent his eldest son, David, over to me to keep me company. It was a good idea. He'd known her almost as well as I did. We toasted her memory over glasses of Coca Cola, which was his favourite tipple, and Southern Comfort, which was mine. Then we went out to places like Howth to play pool, or a snooker club in Drumcondra called Breaks.

Over the following months I felt I needed to change my life. Too many things had happened. The move away from Ballina was the first wrench, the death of my father the second. With my mother gone I needed to get away from everything I associated with her. I thought of her saying to me after he died, 'You're my job now,' and me being confused about what she meant. I was still confused even after she died and was relieved of that job.

She didn't have to go into a convent now either. She was in her own world for once.

I tried to find my one. The teaching job couldn't give it to me and neither could my night life. When I met people with David they seemed like shadows to me. It was the same way they felt like shadows after I left Ballina and after my father died. Each loss meant a different part of the shell of my life was broken. Who could put Humpty Dumpty back together again?

I thought of leaving the job, of leaving Ireland. Mary and myself considered the possibility of living in America or even Africa. Clive made some enquiries about teaching possibilities in Zambia for me. He'd got me into Belvedere all those years ago. He also got Valerie's son George into Fordham University. Could he pull a third string?

Marriage

In the end we decided to stay in Ireland. We sold the house in the Villas the following year. I'd been sixteen years in it, exactly the same amount of time as I'd been in the Ballina Norfolk. It felt longer.

Sean MacDonnell did it up before it went on the market. A few months after it was sold I moved into a flat nearby. Sean stayed with me sometimes. He'd been with me, I thought, in the three main places I lived: Ballina, the Villas and now Claremont.

Mary came over too. We reminisced about happier times with my mother and father, with her own mother and father. Her father had died the same year mine did. Her mother was now in a nursing home.

We decided it was time we got married. We'd been seeing one another one and off since in the seventies. It was a relatively short courtship by Irish standards, only about fifteen years.

Like our parents, we did it quietly. There were just two witnesses. It was a legal requirement. I'd have been happy to just pick two people off the streets. Mary said that would be maybe a bit too bohemian.

We'd spent so long getting ready to tie the knot we wanted the least amount of fuss. We chose a church in Phibsboro near the Cabra Park flat. Afterwards we took a few photos in a field.

'I don't think *Hello* magazine will be looking for the rights to them,' I said to her.

'The people in *Hello* often break up,' she said, 'It should be called *Goodbye*.'

When I showed her mother the wedding ring she said, 'It's very nice. And the woman wearing it isn't too bad either.' She was right about that.

The family were shocked when I told them I'd tied the knot.

'You sneaky thing,' they said. I felt bad for denying them a day out but I'd always hated big splashes.

The teachers at the school were shocked too. I was finally 'cash and carried.' 'It's all downhill from now on,' one of them said to me. I asked him if he was speaking from experience.

Mary was shy like my mother and I was the same way like my father even if that wasn't obvious at first. I was also systematic like Mary's father. She told me I reminded her of him. I told her she reminded me of my mother.

'Every man marries his mother,' she said, 'and every woman marries her father.' I told her that was a bit too oedipal for me but I took her point.

Married life was quiet. As a bachelor I was out most nights. Marriage meant the opposite. I didn't know if it would suit me but habits grow on you.

I became like my father, someone who didn't think he'd take to it but did. After a few months I didn't even want to go out at nights. I didn't know if that was a good or a bad thing. Would I get that 'married' look? Would I fall in love with my chains?

I left teaching soon afterwards. It was getting too much for me. Corporal punishment had been abolished by this time. I'd been a victim of it as a pupil. When it was removed I felt a different kind of victim. The children got cheekier when the threat of the 'bata' was no longer there.

When my father was talking about Albert Pierrepoint, the famous hangman, he said the abolition of capital punishment made criminals more daring. I felt something similar was happening with children now.

I didn't believe in hitting people and he didn't like the idea of anyone being hanged. We were talking about the threat of something giving people a fear of it.

In the end I wasn't able for the job. Children are good psychologists. They know when they're getting the upper hand on you. After a certain point of time they started to affect my health. When you get to that stage of a job it's time to get out.

Keith was feeling the pressure in Unidare too. Around the same time I left my job he left his one. Had I given him the idea? I wasn't sure of that but we were undergoing the same kinds of tensions.

Neither of us had ever been happy in our jobs. Both of us did them because we had to, unlike the other three boys in the family who had vocations of various sorts. Hugo and Clive were totally fulfilled at their teaching. Basil was going a bomb in America.

'Once you're doing something you like,' as the saying goes, 'you'll never have to work again.' Both Keith and I liked to write.

Keith left Unidare to write a book about screenwriters. He would spend the next 25 years of his life finessing it.

Bazil with my mother

Alternatives

I did some courier work after I left teaching. As I went around Dublin with my packages I was reminded of the days in Ballina bringing my father's letters to the other solicitors in the town. I doubted that this kind of life was what he had in mind for me when he said he wanted me to become 'a man of letters.'

Delivering letters was more relaxing than teaching but more physically arduous. The pressure in teaching was mainly psychological. In the courier world it was to do with time. The first time I heard the term 'ASAP' was from a cranky secretary on Ormond Quay.

By now I was doing bits and pieces of journalism for various newspapers and magazines. It meant I was my own boss.

That's not to say I didn't have commitments but I could choose to ignore them if I wanted. Writing wasn't like teaching where you had forty children looking to you for guidance. It wasn't like being a courier where the boss was sending up smoke signals if you didn't get to a particular destination on time.

I wrote the occasional book review for 'The Irish Times.' Maybe it was a vague gesture of loyalty towards my father. I raised a toast to him some nights. I now had a byline in the paper all the 'best people' read. I wondered if he was looking down on me. Maybe he was too busy looking up the words I was using in his celestial dictionary.

I wish he developed his writing side more. He did it in some of the letters he wrote to the 'Times.' On the other hand, if he devoted himself more to writing he mightn't have been able to give as much of himself to life.

Writing separates us from people. I've found that myself. They see you differently and you see them differently. Everything we do in life comes at a price. I never enjoyed books or films as much after I started reviewing them than I did before. Maybe I haven't enjoyed life as much since I started writing about that either. Every book is like an execution of sorts in that sense. We kill the thing we love.

The poems my father wrote had forced rhymes but they still captured his personality:

'When the situation clamours
For a pardonable lie
Please begin your observations with,
'As no one will deny.'

The first verse of another one went,

'We asked not to be born
We do not want to die
We spend our lives malingering
In the vast eternal why.'

The best book he could have written, I always thought, would have been a record of his time. He saw the old world disappearing and the new one coming in. He could have been a chronicler of life at that crossroads.

In the absence of him writing books, I started writing them. Maybe I was trying to make up for him. He gave me my love of words. I owed him that much. Some of them were reviewed in the 'Western People.' The editor, Terry Reilly, and his successor, James Laffey, gave them plugs whenever they could.

My books were trivial at first. They got more serious as they went on. The trivial ones made the most money. That seemed to be the way life worked. Bad books were rewarded. Maybe reviewers were threatened by the good ones. Either that or they became tired of me. I wasn't the new kid on the block anymore.

After a while I felt the writing business was becoming mechanised. Publishers started to ask me how much time I planned to spend promoting my books rather than trying to find out if they were any good or not. I felt I was becoming a supermarket commodity.

'Would you do a signing?' they asked, 'Are there any events coming up where you could advertise it?' If James Joyce was around, I wondered, would he have become famous without a website? Would Van Gogh have sold any of his paintings if he wasn't on Instagram? Probably not. He'd have been too busy cutting his ear off.

I put my father on the cover of a novel I wrote in 1996. It was called 'The Things That Were.'

That was the phrase from 'Lasca' that he loved. I chose a photograph of me with him on Enniscrone beach. He was in his Trinity gear in it. I changed his circumstances for the story, making him into a gentleman farmer in it. A man who knew him as a solicitor in Ballina couldn't get his head around that. When he reviewed it in the 'Western' he said it made him look ridiculous.

He regarded the novel as a biography because of the photo on the cover. I saw his point but in a novel anyone can be anything. I knew that if my father was a farmer he would have been a gentleman one. I doubted he'd have spent much time raising crops.

I could imagine him saying to someone, 'How do you milk a cow?' the same way he said to my mother, 'How do you make a cup of tea?' when she had her migraine.

Some years later I put him on the cover of another book, a poetry collection I called 'Mature Student.' The 'Mature' was meant to be sardonic. He's also been on the cover of many of my Penniless Press books, and on the inside of them as well.

He once said his life would have been more fulfilled if he took silk, if he became a State solicitor, if he was able to say 'M'lud' to a man in a tilted wig in the Old Bailey. I never had any interest in such things. At a certain point I don't think he did either.

I started to miss him more as the years went on. In photographs of him I tried to see if there were resemblances to any of us. People outside the family seemed to be more aware of these than I was.

Patrick Kavanagh once said that every old man he met reminded him of his father. That wasn't the case with me but one night some years ago I met Paddy Dillon-Malone's brother Stephen in the Stag's Head pub in Temple Bar. Both of them were sons of Uncle Louis.

Stephen was more like my father than Paddy in his personality. The longer the night went on the more I felt I was talking to my father rather than Stephen. His eyes danced in his head like my father's did when he told funny stories.

Stephen liked his drink too. He had a hip flask of whiskey with him on the night I met him. He was swigging from it merrily. 'My wife is giving me the devil's eye,' he said at one stage, laughing like a child.

We talked about Paddy. I only met him once after Clive's ordination. It was in 1970. He was driving me out to Louvain, his house in Dundrum. He didn't talk much, apart from a few sentences about my father as we passed TCD. 'Sorry for being anti-social,' he said at one stage in that posh Stoneyhurst voice of his. I didn't know what 'anti-social' meant.

Even though Paddy was different from Stephen, he was more like him than either of them were like Uncle Louis. Both of them had vulnerability and both had the DM nerves. I was always more attracted to that than strength. When Hugo talked about Marlon Brando I thought about James

Dean. When he talked about John F. Kennedy I thought about his brother Robert. Lost sheep were always more interesting than found ones.

How would I have turned out if I was Uncle Louis' son? What would I have looked like if I crossed O'Connell Bridge with my wife in 1935 on the cusp of responsibility? Would I have had the same worried look my father had ? Would I have been able to deal with the fall-out from the end of my party lifestyle and the beginning of a career in a town of 600 people and eight solicitors?

I'd probably have struggled like my father did, but in that struggle I'd hopefully have found deeper reserves in myself like he did too.

Uncle Louis didn't have to search for those reserves. They were always there inside him. Paddy did, which caused him to have far too short a life.

He died soon after I met him in 1970. He was only 42, the same age as Elvis when he 'left the building.' Two lonely souls were gone too soon.

The good die young.

My parents on O'Connell Bridge

Contrasts

The more I talked to Stephen the more I became aware of the contrast between my father and Paddy, of the contrast between him and Uncle Louis. I thought of Uncle Louis with his sensible life and his sensible life and his sensible career in sensible England with his nuclear family of three, just a third of my father's tally. There was also a girl, Mary. Neither my father nor Uncle Louis named any of their sons after them. This may be significant.

Paddy named one of his sons Hugo, perhaps after my father. He also had a daughter, Louise, presumably named after Uncle Louis. Some years ago she wrote a book about all the famous writers who'd written about fatherhood, all the way from Shakespeare to Dickens.

She also wrote about her own reminiscences of Paddy, about the way he used to sing *camáille* songs to her sometimes when she was young and he was feeling frivolous. It was a bit like when my father sang them, when he was being really himself, when his defences were down with drink or just feeling merry. Maybe they were more alike than we realised.

That was nine children versus three. The difference between Ireland and England. If you had a big family, as the saying went, you were either a good Catholic or a bad Protestant. If you had a small one you were either a bad Catholic or a good Protestant.

I always thought of Uncle Louis as being more like a Protestant than a Catholic, not only because he went to England but because of his personality. If I was one of his children I imagined myself growing up in a quiet house, doing my homework at the prescribed time every day and going to bed at the same time every night, even having my play time supervised.

When I reached the required age I'd have been 'put down' for somewhere like Oxford or Cambridge or indeed Stoneyhurst. I'd join all the other children of privilege in the groves of academe, emerging after three or four years with a piece of paper that would entitle me to practise medicine in Harley Street or law in the Old Bailey. As I was doing so, maybe my father would tell me tales of his brother in Ballina with his Roscommon wife and his horde of children. And so the circle would turn, each brother pursuing his goals in his own way. If I'd been that child would I have grown up like Paddy or Stephen?

Stephen always thought Paddy's main problem was that he went into the wrong line of work. He became a businessman instead of an academic, which was his true calling. He tried his best to make it interesting but it was never going to in the long run, even though he expanded the business world into a visionary area with his great imagination.

As I listened to him I thought of myself, of my changing from Commerce into Arts. Then I thought of my father. Had he made a mistake in his career too? Would he have been happier as an academic? Did he retire too soon? How would he have been if he stayed in Ballina? Would he have become more depressed or less? Did he only imagine he was fed up of the law when he decided to retire? Was he wise to take himself away from everything he knew in the town? Should he have gone down there at all in the first place?

I thought of the photograph of him crossing O'Connell Bridge with my mother. Her hair was dark in it. I never knew her with dark hair. She was wearing a kind of Garbo hat and smiling, as always.

My father had his Trinity tie on and a handkerchief in his lapel. He was looking worried as he clutched his umbrella. There was so much worry even in those days. Was he thinking of his new life in Ballina, of all the ways it would change his life? After he died I found something pulling me back to the town, some invisible force. It was as if it was my last link to him, to that part of him I wanted to know more about.

I went back to it every now and then in the following years. It was as if it held some key to him, some explanation of who he was and what he became. Every time I crossed the Shannon it was with a sense of excitement. Oliver Cromwell said 'To Hell or to Connacht' but to me it was more like heaven. I thought of how different I was from my father in my attitude. He couldn't wait to leave it and I couldn't wait to get back to it. Maybe that was because he spent too many years there and me not enough.

My first few trips were enjoyable but then the people I knew began to drift away. Their departure made me feel more like a tourist instead of someone who used to live there. I started to feel like the Elvis song, 'a stranger in my own home town.'

Most of the people my father knew were dead. The next generation, my one, were either gone to other places or were inaccessible. Some of them were in Dublin but I didn't know what part. Often I didn't care enough about them to look them up.

Aunt Nellie was usually my first port of call. She had more cats than ever now. Her hearing had got bad with the years. I rapped on the door many times but she rarely heard me. She was often upstairs. If she was, it was a question of throwing pebbles at the upstairs window.

One year I got the idea of going to the phone box across the road from her, the one outside Jimmy Geraghty's shop. I felt ringing her would give her less of a fright than tapping on the window. Her curtains were open as I dialled her number. I watched her picking the receiver up. I said, 'I'm across the road.' She said, 'Who's speaking?'

I met some old stagers from Muredach's who'd stayed in the town. We shot the breeze about old times but soon ran out of steam. After recycling a few anecdotes about the teachers we had little to talk about. Maybe we'd all become too sensible. Maturity meant boredom. There was more excitement in the confusions of adolescence.

Often I don't know what I was looking for on these trips. I went into Norfolk on most of them. The first time I entered the house I spent ages in each room trying to dig up memories. I went into the dining room where we had our Christmas dinner each year, where my father's office was, where he entertained us with stories, popping his monocle out as he got to the punchlines. Then I went into the sitting room where my mother used to play the piano.

When I went upstairs I couldn't believe how small the landing was. I felt I could nearly touch the four walls if I stretched my hands out.

The bedrooms seemed small too. So did the boxroom, but then that always was. I thought of all the hours I spent there looking out the window at the fire station, thinking the thing every boy dreams when he's young, that he'll be a fireman when he grows up. Maybe I could have put out the fire in my father's office that time if I was one.

I remembered the old school, the place where they made headstones. I thought of dropping trays onto the street with Ann O'Grady to frighten people passing by. How we didn't give them heart attacks I'll never know.

Mark Twain once said that when we go back to the place where we grew up it's our youth we're looking for rather than the place. Maybe he's right. Anytime I passed by Norfolk I thought of the line from 'Rebecca:' 'Last night I dreamt I went to Manderley.' Sometimes I passed by it without going in. At a certain point I began to be afraid of the memories it called up. What good were they if you couldn't do anything about them?

Every time I went back to Ballina it seemed to be retreating farther and farther away from me. The buildings looked different and so did the streets. People I'd known didn't even look like themselves anymore.

Was this the town's punishment to me for leaving it? I felt like someone looking at a star that was already fallen. I knew from my Science classes in Muredach's that stars took many light years to travel to us so when we looked at them they mightn't be there anymore.

Could I ever get it back or was the problem inside myself? 'The moving finger wrote,' as my father said, 'and having writ moved on.'

It would have been nice if he could have been with me on these trips, to go down to Leigue again, or up Primrose Hill like Basil's ducklings, or even to the courthouse, the scene of those victories that seemed so tumultuous in the absence of anything else.

These were forlorn wishes. The past had receded beyond reach. The more I tried to trick it into being, the farther it drifted away. It was like a beach ball in the sea, like footprints in the sand. Trying to call it back was no more than masochism. I'd be in danger of turning the town into a pillar of salt, like Lot's wife.

The first time I went back it was like an intravenous injection of nostalgia. Every street called up a memory. Then I stopped going for some years. People thought I didn't care about it, that I was getting on with my life now, more focussed on the future than the past, but maybe the truth of the matter was that I cared too much.

Maybe I was like Ruth in Jersey, afraid to come home in case she'd find it difficult to go back again. Even though it hadn't been a part of my life for years it was still lodged in my subconscious like the amputated limb of a person who still felt pain in the area where it used to be. That was what thinking about it did to me. I had to stop before it took me over.

One year when I went down there, the Market Square was gone. A supermarket was built there. The place where we played football for hours on end, like Croke Park without grass, was nothing now, its great space eaten up by shoppers. What was next, I wondered. Was anywhere safe from developers?

Norfolk eventually became the Ballina Community Centre. The advantage of that was that you could go in anytime you wanted. The bad part was that anyone else could as well.

Various organisations held meetings there, including Alcoholics Anonymous. My father would have been amused at that. I remembered him telling me there were more pubs in Ballina than any other town in the county. Maybe it was a statistical inevitability that we'd turn out more alcoholics than the average town.

My mother's riding colours were long gone from the outside of the house now. So was my father's plaque. Such changes took away my sentiment for it.

I don't know if that's a good or a bad thing. In one of my visits I took solace from the fact that some of the light fittings hadn't changed since 1969. Such details seemed to matter to me. They were a link to the past.

On other visits I thought of him going through his files, putting them on the shelves of the dining room so we could play table tennis. I thought of him ordering cups of tea through The Hatch, of him asking people to swear on the Bible as he signed documents for them. I thought of him pinning them to the wall as he unleashed anecdote after anecdote on them, his monocle popping out as he got to the punchlines.

After meeting Stephen I started to see him in other people I met, people I knew well and people I didn't. Sometimes they took on his characteristics. As I talked to them I felt myself back in his time. I heard his voice and his laughter. I heard him telling me that my world didn't hold a candle to his one. More often than not I found myself agreeing with him.

Most people who knew him saw him as little more than his image. When they met any of the family they talked about his apparel, his oratory, his ability to work a room. They didn't know what he was like when he closed the door of Norfolk, when he became just another man to us, someone coming home after a day's work, or coming into the kitchen for a chat.

Aunt Nellie died some years afterwards. I went down to Ballina for her funeral. Paddy Murphy organised it. He was aware that it was the end of an era.

'All the Dillon-Malones are gone from the town now,' he said. These were hard words for me to hear.

I saw some familiar faces at the funeral Mass. They talked fondly about her. I remembered my father saying how he loved her from a distance, how they were 'cut from a different cloth.' Like him she was a 'character,' one of the few remaining in our increasingly bland world.

After her house was sold it was pulled down and a petrol station built in its place. That seemed to say it all to me about how the town was losing its identity. I'd never see Feamore House again. I'd never see Aunt Nellie playing with her cats or laughing that giddy laugh of hers or asking after 'Red Hugh.'

The world changed in the 1990s. The Celtic Tiger started to roar. Ireland became the style capital of Europe. House prices rose to ridiculous levels. Shacks in the bad end of Dublin started selling for seven figure sums.

Mary and myself considered selling Viking Road for a while. I thought of my father saying of my grandfather, 'He knew when to buy and when to sell, that was his secret.' No matter how many recessions there were, bricks and mortar always held their value.

He never had to make those kinds of decisions himself, feeling fortunate in having one roof over his head rather than two or more. I was glad he was that kind of a father rather than a cute businessman.

Mary's mother used to say you could only live in one house at a time and eat one meal at a time. Apart from Uncle Eddie I never knew any rich people I liked. It always seemed to me that they spent more time worrying about money than the poor. When someone devoted their lives to building a fortune, other things usually suffered. At their limit they became someone like King Midas – or Donald Trump.

I never saw my father haggling with anyone over a business deal. It wasn't his style. If he got a cut from Jimmy Geraghty on our grocery bill it was unbidden, a case of 'noblesse oblige.' If we got presents from Benny Walkin or free tickets to the Estoria from Paddy Mulligan it was because he did something for them in return.

On my last trip to Ballina I tried to see him the way people outside the family did. I imagined him walking up Arthur Street to the courthouse, passing the Estoria and the font and the crazy pavement beside it, walking across Bury Street and entering the court, building himself up for a performance, becoming for an hour or so a barrister instead of a solicitor as he magnified an insignificant case into something much larger by his words, using his persuasive skills to soften a judge.

I imagined him in the Downhill Hotel entertaining people with stories of Blackrock and Castleknock. He would have been taking out the photographs of all of us at the end of such nights, flashing them around to people who wouldn't have known us from Adam as they scampered from the bar to get away from him.

People often ask me if he had a problem with drink. I tell them it wasn't drink that was the problem, it was life. He was sensitive and sensitive people need some protection from that life, especially if they feel it's let them down. They see drink as giving them that protection, as bringing them to a kind of higher reality.

Humphrey Bogart used to say the world was 'three drinks behind.' He saw sobriety as the problem. When he was drinking he felt himself on a higher plane, in touch with something beautiful. With my father that plane was his past. The problem was when he had to trade in that past for the dullness of the present. In that sense it was like a time machine for him.

I never got to talk to him about things like that. Why do we spend so much of our lives exchanging trivia instead of going into the things that really matter?

I never told him I loved him. I didn't tell my mother either. I don't remember hugging either of them except maybe after a trip away. I never sent him a Father's Day card or my mother a Mother's Day one. We weren't conscious of the fact that our father were our fathers then, or our mothers were our mothers. They existed in a different Ireland, one where hugging your parents wasn't required by law, as seems to be the case today. They were just there, like a fact of nature, like the rock of Gibralter.

Not telling people you love them doesn't mean you don't. Telling them you do a hundred times a day is more like Hollywood. 'Love you,' is a phrase that's trotted out today more times than is good for people, especially when so many more relationships are breaking down at the rate of knots.

Mary sometimes tells me I remind her of my father. When we flew to Jersey one year I certainly shared his terror of airplanes. There was so much turbulence on the flight I vowed never to leave 'terra firma' again.

I share his claustrophobia as well, and the feeling of vertigo he used to have on the balcony in the Estoria. When I'm on a cliff with Mary I usually ask her to stand downside of me.

I spent sixteen years with him in Ballina but only half that amount of time in Dublin. They say our early years form us. I think that's true with me. I see myself as his Ballina son rather than his Dublin one.

I never saw myself as a Dubliner, even an adoptive one. I could never shout for the Dublin football team no matter how many years I've spent here. The Mayo one, they say, is cursed never to win an All-Ireland.

I don't know whether such a curse is the result of disrespect shown to a priest in 1951, as legend has it, when the members of our last winning team were coming home from Croke Park, or something internal. I see it as a mental block that makes us feel we're not as good as anyone else. My father's famous 'inferiority complex.'

Dublin won six All-Irelands some years ago when they were managed by Jim Gavin, the so-called 'baby-faced killer' who withdrew so dramatically from the presidential election recently, in the process showing himself to be a much more vulnerable individual than he appeared to be when he was leading the Dubs to their six-in-a-row. Mayo, meanwhile, are still chasing that elusive single title after a 75-year drought.

Why does the 'Sam' continue to be so precious to them – and to me – despite all our frustrations at Croke Park? Maybe for that very reason. It's the forbidden fruit, like Ballina.

I forget our phone number in Iona Villas but I still remember our Ballina one, 143. Is this another subconscious suppression of the Villas years on my part? Did I refuse to let it become important to me? Did I stubbornly resist its efforts to become the new Ballina?

I didn't go to the 50th anniversary of the Belvedere Past Pupils Union when it was held in 2020. I doubt my father would have approved of my decision. He'd have wanted me to be an old Belvederian rather than an ex-Muredach's person.

I knew I could never be that. It wasn't just the fact that I'd only spent a year there. It was that Dublin wasn't in my DNA any more than it was in his.

No matter how many monocles he put in his eye or any many pinstriped suits he wore, he was a country person to the core. He might have needed to leave Ballina when he did but he spent most of his life there. That has to have an effect.

He had a love-hate relationship to the town just like I had. Love and hate are close to one another. They both indicate passion.

It's our early years that form us. Oaks come from acorns. The child is father of the man. You can take the man out of the bog but you can't take the bog out of the man.

Inheritance

My father didn't leave me any official inheritance when he died but I inherited a lot of characteristics from him.

He pre-dated the era of the 'Super Dad.' He pre-dated the era of 'Growing up with your children,' 'Getting to know them at each stage of their development' and all the other bromides you see trotted out in the trendy Sunday supplements. These are usually written by 'relationship counsellors' who probably know as much about parenting as a pig knows about a holiday, to use an expression of John O'Grady's.

He pre-dated the New Dads one sees on television yammering on about how they cut the umbilical cord of their firstborn, how they suffered morning sickness in empathy with their pregnant partners, how they applied for paternity leave from their jobs so they could witness 'Junior's' first steps and first words, how they went to pre-natal classes with the aforementioned partners, how they huffed and puffed with them on mats borrowed from the lady who was doing Pilates in the room next door.

He never told me to brush my teeth or tidy my room or do my lessons or said I was playing music too loud or told me to take my hands out of my pockets or to walk straighter or to not walk on the grass or to not use bad language.

He never told me I looked or dressed badly or told me to eat my vegetables at dinner.

He never brought me to a circus or a carnival but I didn't need him to. The main circuses and carnivals of my youth were in Norfolk.

He never played football with me. If he did, he'd probably have fallen over the ball. He didn't build sandcastles for me in Enniscrone or identify seashells with me. I didn't expect him to. It was enough that he was there.

He never told me he had superior knowledge to me about anything. There was a programme we watched in Ballina in the fifties called 'Father Knows Best.' I didn't want him to be that person and he didn't want to be him either.

The arc of his life went from party animal to family man to Il Penseroso. I watched him turning from the 'Anyone for tennis' persona of TCD to the brooding Hamlet crossing O'Connell Bridge with my mother to his last personality of our own King Lear, raging against the elements as time's winger chariot gained on him. In all of these phases he was intensely himself. That was the thing that resonated about him. No matter how many times he reinvented himself there was always a connecting thread.

The past hung on to him like the ends of his cigarettes, like the bottoms of his whiskey glasses. He felt he could touch it if he tried hard enough, like F. Scott Fitzgerald's Jay Gatsby, or James Joyce's Greta Conroy, or Chekhov's Three Sisters.

Why was it so magical for him? Was it because it didn't exist anymore? Was that why he went to so many lengths to recapture it? But the harder he tried, the more it receded from him. In the end he was beaten by time, as most of us are.

The more I think of him, the more I think of the expression, 'He who searches for God has already found him.' Even though he's gone, he isn't.

My search for him might be the search of all sons for their fathers, or their ultimate father.

That was Freud's theory of religion. Here in Ireland we saw it in people like De Valera and John Charles McQuaid. Sometimes people say that when the British left Ireland we needed new authority figures and we found them in the church.

That was Ireland as it used to be. The new Ireland doesn't seem to have a need of any authority figures, be it in politics or religion or anywhere else. We become our own Gods, our own figureheads.

One of the first books I read in UCD was 'Atheism and Alienation.' Such words wouldn't even have been uttered in Ballina, never mind talked about. At that time atheism was a curiosity. Now it's become the norm. 'God is dead,' said Nietzsche. In many people's minds he is. But if he was alive once, surely he has to be alive forever.

Nietzsche spoke of him as a human being. He was that, but what about the other part of him? Nietzsche was a poet rather than a theologian. These are questions to which there are no answers. There's only how you feel. Martin Luther said faith was located under the left nipple. I know what he meant.

With the death of a religious God we probably witness the death of all other gods as well, the gods of politics or education or the law or any other institution where authority once held sway.

We've replaced them with the kind of pagan indulgences we see about us today everywhere we look. My father liked G.K. Chesteron. He often quoted him. And as I said, he named Keith after him.

Chesterton once said, 'When people stop believing in God they don't believe in nothing. They believe in anything.' So we have the Tarot card God, the pop music god, the film god, the 'Star Wars' god. 'Did God make man,' my father once queried, 'or did man make God?'

He loved questioning things like that. I shared his sense he had that something isn't right with the world, that the odds were stacked against us as soon as we were born. Accepting that, we both agreed, helped us get through life. If we bridled against it, it only made things worse.

I liked his sense of the absurdity of life. He thought our biggest weapon over it was to make fun of that. As Samuel Beckett said, when you're in the last ditch, all you can do is sing.

I like to question things like my father did. Some of these questions come out of my head and some out of books. I read a lot of books like he did, often a few at a time. That was another habit of his, that I inherited, stacking books up everywhere and thumbing through them here and there. I also like quotations in the same way he did.

I'm shy like him too and often feel out of place at events. Like him I blow hot and cold with people. I often fail to count to ten when they upset me.

In the days when I used to smoke I got more nicotine on my hands than in my lungs like he did. Maybe that's what saved him from 'the big C.'

Why did my mother get it and not him? Who knows the answer to any of these questions.

'That old cancer,' she said when it came back. It was almost as if it was a person she was talking about. She put up with it like she put up with everything in life, seeing it as a Grand Plan on the part of God: 'Whom the Lord loveth he chastiseth.'

There are other similarities between myself and my father. I type with two fingers like he did, for instance, generally doing my best to break the sound barrier in the process.

I like children even though I never had any of my own. I think rugby should be outlawed by the Constitution. When it comes to dancing I have two left feet.

I'm also a technophobe like he was, and as perplexed by things other people can do in their sleep, even people my own age. I also inherited a hoarding instinct from him. Other people's fathers collected coins or vintage cars. Mine collected pieces of paper and so do I.

I'm also bad with technology like he was. I can make a cup of tea and boil an egg but not much beyond that. I don't set mattresses on fire like he did but if you asked me to cook a meal I'd probably burn every pot in the house.

I can't perform even the most simple mechanical tasks on my car. I once tried to open the petrol tank of my last one with a kitchen knife.

Both my father and I often wrote letters that got us into trouble, sometimes to the papers. And I enjoy a drink. Like him I have a love-hate relationship to Ballina. Like him I was spoiled by my mother. Like him I suffer from vertigo and claustrophobia.

Like him I went through a lot of confusion in university, not having a clear vision of what my future might be when I was there.

I became doubtful about everything in middle age like he did, eventually concluding that very few things make sense in life.

And I never grew up.

Endings

Keith died in 2014. It was like the last element of my father disappearing from my life. I thought of him discussing films with him, or horses, or the nerves they both suffered from. Keith knew him better than anyone, from Fuschia Cottage to the two Norfolks, from his first days as a solicitor to his retirement, the two poles of his existence. He saw him in all his moods but never judged him.

They were birds of a feather from their first day to their last. I often envied Keith knowing him in the first days of his marriage, witnessing him moving from the house on Convent Hill to the one on Arthur Street, bringing him to the forties films in the Estoria, being with him on the Primrose Hill walks, seeing him as a thin man with wiry hair before he became the 'character' of his middle age, the man Sean Bocht described as 'gracefully growing old.'

He never got to be a state solicitor and Keith never got his screenwriter book out. How many lives are characterised by these what-might-have-beens? Marlon Brando said that of all the films he made, the scene most people wanted to talk to him about was the 'I coulda bin a contendah' one from *On the Waterfront.* Maybe we're all on that one-way ticket to Palookaville. Maybe we're all, like Uncle Michael, putting our money on the wrong horse in life, watching it fall at the last fence instead of making us rich.

Keith's home in Artane is gone now too. Jacqueline went into a nursing home a year ago. Clive used to stay there when he came home. Now he can't. We've all had to change our arrangements.

People from the family still come home from America but it isn't like it used to be. In the old days there was one place they all stayed. When we meet now, it's anywhere and everywhere.

There have also been other deaths in the family. All of my sisters lost their husbands. This happened over a number of years but that doesn't make it any easier to bear. Such tragedies have even extended into a different generation with the shocking death of Keith's son Derek some years ago.

Derek was a lovely lad. Nobody ever had a bad word to say about him. He was a loving father too, leaving many children behind him who mourn him deeply. His life was short but he left a mark on everyone who met him. I've often thought he was too gentle for this world. As Hemingway said, 'Life breaks everyone and afterwards some are strong at the broken places.' Others it brutalises too badly to recover.

Derek wrote a beautiful tribute to my mother after she died. He knew her from our later days at Iona Villas. Unfortunately he didn't know my father. If he did, I know he'd have liked him. They had the same sense of fun.

The death of Keith and the scattering of his sons to the four winds was like a metaphor for the splitting up of the rest of us. We don't see one another as much as we used to these days. When we do, it's often in different places to our homes. Some of the time, sadly, it's at funerals, the so-called cocktail parties of the geriatric set. Where once it was automatic that there would be gatherings at the 'old hacienda,' now the family meet up in different towns, different cities, even different continents.

Things are even more complicated when it comes to the next generation. Audrey and Jacinta sometimes have to fly thousands of miles to see their children and grandchildren. Jacinta went from one state to another to be with them. Basil drives upstate in New York to see his. Audrey had to go all the way to Australia to be with hers. June went to London to visit her daughter. My father didn't live long enough to see his grandchildren growing up. What a pity.

The world is a global village now. That applies to the family members who stayed in Ireland as well as for those who left it. Hugo has become more immersed in his world in Goatstown over the last number of years. Basil and Clive have retired but keep active. Mary is out a lot. I'm more reclusive. Each of us has their comfort zones, their priorities. We've grown into the people we always were as children even if we didn't know it then. As Jacinta says, we've become more of who we are.

With the exception of Keith, we all exceeded our parents' age when they died. I don't know if this is due to the fact that we've taken better care of ourselves or simply that people are living longer today than they used to. That's one of the few good things about the modern world. Now I'm beginning to sound like my father.

What would he make of all of us? What would he make of the world we live in? It was a mystery to him when he was alive and would probably be even more so to him now that there's so much diversity in our lives.

There was a time when a long journey was the three hours on the train from Ballina to Dublin. That's about the same time it takes to get from Dublin to New York. The more often that trip is made, the more casual people feel about it.

I didn't think of my father much anytime I was in America in my young days. For that matter, I didn't think of my mother much during these times either. That's the arrogance of youth. We imagine we're the centre of the universe and that our parents are stuck in some kind of cement back home. We usually only rid ourselves of these feelings when we reach the age they were when we were busy forgetting them.

I'm not forgetting them anymore. 'Memory is the only friend that grief can call its own,' he used to say. That memory is my own friend now too.

I indulged it mainly whenever I went back to Ballina. That wasn't half often enough. When I was there I didn't go to the hotels he went to. I preferred the bars. I felt he was more himself in these than the plush places.

Neither did I go to the Spars and Centras and all the other identikit convenience stores that were springing up everywhere. I preferred going to places like Cafolla's, the café across the street from his old office. After a few minutes there I always felt like I'd never left the town. It preserved its flavour by not trying. You'd see people coming in with bags of potatoes, people with lived-in faces and lived-in clothes.

I didn't visit the family vault anytime I was down there or look up his genealogical chart in the library. I had little interest in things like that. Instead I just walked the streets to try and find his spirit in them – the street down to his old office, the one that led to the courthouse, the one going across the bridge to Bunree, the one we lived on where his new office was after the old one burned down.

In 2020 I planned to go down to Ballina for the 50th anniversary of my Leaving Cert class in Muredach's. Even though I didn't do the exam down there I was still invited. I was looking forward to the event but then Covid struck and it was cancelled. It was like the time in 1977 when I applied for teaching practice in Ballina and the roads became frozen over. Some malign deity seemed to be blocking my path across the Shannon every time I got an opportunity to do something concrete down there.

I've had a number of books published since he died. The more I got out, the more I wanted. I never thought of myself as being ambitious when I was young. In Muredach's or in the teaching job it was like a case of getting through the day without a crisis. But when I found something I liked doing I wanted more of it. The effort wasn't really in the writing but in getting things placed. It was like the old saying, 'If you find something you like doing you'll never have to work again.'

Maybe it was the same with my father's studying in Trinity. It was a slog to him because he had no personal connection to it. That changed after he met my mother. He had a motivation now. After they went back to Ballina he found he enjoyed being a father. That gave him even more motivation.

I wonder what he'd have made of my books. Sometimes I read memoirs of sons who've gone on to achieve things after their father passed away. They usually say something like, 'I wish Dad lived to see my success. It would have meant so much to him.' What they're really saying is how brilliant they think they are. It isn't a thought about their fathers as much as about themselves.

It was a shock to me when he died but when I think of his passing these days it's almost with a sense of relief. He didn't have much to look forward to at the time he died. The changes he saw coming wouldn't have suited him.

He didn't live to see the clerical scandals. He didn't live to see solicitors sleeping in cars because they couldn't afford to buy homes in modern Ireland.

He didn't live to see people from the wrong side of the tracks playing rugby. He didn't live to see answering machines or mobile phones or microwave ovens or carbon footprints or botox or people putting so many tattoos on their bodies that you could hardly see their skin anymore.

I can't imagine him ever sending a text or an email if he lived until that era. If he did, it would probably have been longer than *War and Peace*.

I'm sure he knew about George Orwell's *Big Brother*. He didn't live to see its trivialisation in a game show that exerted an addictive attraction for me in the early years of this century when I found some kind of crazy empathy in watching its contestants as I pitted the mediocrity of my life against the even greater mediocrity of theirs.

He didn't see car boot sales or bouncy castles or negative equity or the squeezed middle or GUBU or AI or data protection or Riverdance or political correctness or the Celtic Tiger and its Armageddon-style collapse.

He didn't see a world where 'anti-social' behaviour didn't refer to someone not wanting to go to a party but rather telling people you were going to slice their head open with a drill. If he thought the world he lived in was bad, he was lucky not to have seen the one that followed it.

He didn't see Blu-Rays or DVDs or even videos. He didn't see the trolley crisis in our hospitals, a crisis that would have made Uncle Louis turn in his grave.

He didn't see tsunamis or the hole in the ozone layer or 9/11 or the wars in Iraq or Afghanistan or the Ukraine or Gaza and their horrific consequences.

He saw a man walking on the moon but not one playing golf on it. Did he miss anything? Sean MacDonnell told me we'd be taking weekend holidays up there some day. Maybe we will, at least if Richard Branson has his way.

He didn't witness the demonic monstrosities of Benjamin Netanyahu and Donald Trump. When the terrorist group Hamas invaded Israel it seemed to me like the answer to a prayer for Netanyahu. It paved the way for him to get what he always wanted, the elimination of Palestine.

The killing of the politician Charlie Kirk a few years later was like the answer to a prayer for Trump. It enabled him to rant on even more about the evils of the left than he'd been doing since he got into office. To those who say he deserved credit for ending the war in Gaza I say he should have ended it two years ago and saved 50,000 lives. I was more heartened by the softening of his attitude towards Zelensky and his promise to get the Ukraine 'done.'

I don't know if my father would have agreed with me on these matters. I regretted the fact that he wasn't alive to debate them with me. He always respected my views like I did his. When we differed in our views, it was amicably.

When I first knew him I was a child and he was a man. At that time he was just a voice, a presence in a pin-striped suit that I watched from a distance from The Hatch, from the table tennis table in the dining room, from the door of Norfolk as he pranced down Arthur Street swinging his umbrella.

As I grew, and grew apart from him intellectually, we started to spar with one another. In time I came to welcome such sparring. I think he did too. He liked arguments if they were friendly. At the end of his life I like to think I was like the solicitors who crossed sabres with him in similarly friendly fashion in the Downhill Hotel and Hursts and Tony Crane's or wherever else he held court as he tried to stem the flow of modernity.

What would he have thought about Putin and Netanyahu? Would they have reminded him of a little man with a toothbrush moustache in Germany in the late thirties? I remember him talking about the annexation of Belgium during World War I, about the rights of small nations, about the disembowelments of Dachau.

Putin he would have seen as yet another example of the dreaded hammer and sickle inching its way outwards from the Iron Curtain. He told me once that the Russian leader Alexander the Great was alleged to have cried once when he had no more lands to conquer.

The war in Ukraine would have brought him back to the Bay of Pigs, an incident even I remember despite being just eight when it happened, the world teetering on the brink as Khruschev tested the mettle of John F. Kennedy, the so-called playboy president.

He didn't get to see Aids or the Ebola virus or Sars or foot and mouth disease or Covid. He didn't witness the depravity to which society can sink or the great heights to which it can soar with technology. He didn't see DNA replacing fingerprints to catch criminals. That was the way they were caught in the Edgar Wallace books he read. How could he have envisaged anything different before the old world faded away and the new one came in?

All that remains of him for me today is photographs. As we get older we look at these kinds of images more and more. When we're young we anticipate. When we're old we reminisce. It's like they say in America about clocks at Halloween, 'Spring forward, fall back.'

For years after I left Ballina I thought it was out of my system. It was only years later I realised the influence it exerted on me would probably never go away. The problem with suppressing feelings is that they become more powerful when they re-assert themselves. Sometimes, as in my father's case, they threaten to engulf the present.

That was one of the reasons I tried to go back to Ballina as much as I could after I left it. It was a way of trying to pacify such memories, like phoning a girlfriend you'd fallen out of love with to keep her from hounding you. Ballina became my guilty pleasure as the years went on just as Trinty did my father's. It was a place I needed to visit more than wanted to. With each trip down there I felt I was burning some more of the need for it out of myself. It was like a kind of chemotherapy of the soul. Maybe my father felt the same about Trinity.

I can never ask him these kinds of questions now. Maybe he wouldn't know the answers to them. Maybe it doesn't really matter either way.

I don't have any moving images of him to clarify him for me, or even tape recordings of his voice. I look at the photographs every now and then to see if I can spot character traits in them that I associate with him.

Most of them are from the years I knew him. These aren't as interesting to me as the ones that were taken before I was born. I find myself looking at these with more fascination, wondering what he was thinking of when they were taken, what future he was planning for himself, how he viewed the people he was with.

I'll never know the answers to these questions. In the absence of that knowledge, the jigsaw of impressions I've drawn up in this book will have to do.

I tell myself he means more to me in my lack of knowledge of him than he would if I knew everything, just like the moon is more beautiful when it's surrounded by clouds than when you see it beaming down at you with nothing near it.

I wonder what he'd think of my life now. He'd probably be glad I'm not a 'National Tramp' anymore. He'd hardly be over the moon about the fact that I wrote a book about Hemingway.

Sometimes he got frustrated about the fact that he didn't know what the future held. He shouldn't have. None of us know that. If we pretend to, we're either snake oil salesmen or weather forecasters.

At the end of the day we're left with nothing but questions. Will the world burn up? Will Trump press the button? Will Covid wipe us all out or will we just die of boredom from watching soaps?

Is life a joke, as he thought sometimes, or a cosmic plan on the part of an omniscient deity who sends global catastrophes our way to test our faith? Was my father right to want to put him in the witness box or would God have dodged his questions by pleading the Fifth?

Is free will a reality or an illusion perpetrated by *fin-de-siecle* psychologists on correspondence courses? Does the devil exist or does it just seem like that when we watch CNN?

Is there intelligent life on other planets or should we devote ourselves to trying to find it on this one? In the next world, presuming there is one, will my father be upstairs with his Harp or downstairs with his Guinness?

The decay of society that he predicted came about much worse than he predicted. If he thought the world was bad when he was alive, what would he think now? If he lived longer, the drawer that was supposedly stuffed with his ramblings in the 'Irish Times' would probably have to be extended to wardrobe size. He'd probably have been able to fill its entire pages with what Jonathan Swift called 'savage indignation.' But maybe the paper wouldn't be interested in publishing them. In the past few decades it came to epitomise many of the very things he spent his life inveighing against.

Most people in the family have a different attitude to my father than I have. I don't claim to know him better than any of them. Maybe I don't know him half as well as they do. When it comes down to it, who can say anyone knows anyone? We all witnessed him at different phases of his life. I saw him in the last quarter of it, at a time when his mood changes were probably more extreme. It made me see his light and shade more stridently.

He had the heart of a liberal inside the head of a conservative, his actions often belying his words. He tried to be tougher than he was sometimes but we never fell for it. At such times he was a sheep in wolf's clothing.

Sometimes I think of the contrast between him and Uncle Louis, one of them travelling on a linear line through life, the other turning this way and that. I don't think my father would have lasted five minutes as a doctor. Being a patient was stressful enough for him. When he looked at the faculties in Trinity before he took up Law, he told me, Medicine was the first one he ruled out.

Having nerves made him more human. Admitting to them made him even more human still. We had a family joke that if he was in bed with my mother and they heard a noise in the kitchen in the middle of the night, she'd be the one more likely to investigate it. He said, 'I'd be fine about that, but who'd protect me when she was out there?' He never minded poking fun at himself like that. His bravery came out in different ways, in how he fought his demons with his head held high.

Courage, Hemingway said, isn't about not having fears. It's about how you deal with them. Bravery, in other words, can't exist without fear.

Now

I don't claim to have given a comprehensive picture of my father in these pages My memories of him are confused with the things that were going on in my life when I had these memories. Sometimes the things got so mixed up with them they coloured them just like litmus paper assumes the colour of what's put into it.

He had a court case once that concerned a car crash. There were three eye witnesses to it. All three of them had different versions of what happened. 'Imagine,' he said, 'if that accident was the dawn of creation. How many people would have seen it in a different way?'

Whenever I look at the photograph of him that I keep on my mantelpiece I think of how he started life as one kind of person and then became another, the cavalier student of the twenties morphing into his philosophical side as the thirties came in.

We only become philosophers when we experience pain. When he was living life to the full he wasn't thinking about that. Which of us would? It was only when he got off the treadmill that he started to brood. Having to deal with a life of responsibility was as tough for him as it was for anyone else who had things easy growing up.

He might have thought he'd only have one child before he got married. 'I wanted to have one to prove I could,' he said to me once. 'You certainly did that,' I said.

Sometimes I felt guilty about being his ninth one. Even though every child was a surprise to parents in an era before family planning, I felt I was extra surprising coming three years after Jacinta. It was at a time when he could have done without the extra expense. How could he have known that eight more children would follow after Keith? Life, as John

Lennon said, is what happens when we're busy making other plans.

When I think of the way his life went I see his move back to Norfolk from Bridge Street in 1966 as being the first step in his retirement. It gave him the idea that being in the house all day mightn't be such a bad thing. He'd raised his children. He always said he'd retire when we were 'set up,' whatever that meant.

I was only 13 then. It would have been better if I was 21 but life doesn't work that way, as Lennon said. Because he was getting tired of Ballina it was almost like he was putting an exit strategy in place. It was time to call time on a place that had little to offer him anymore. He clipped his wings like a bird at rest, asking little of Dublin but that it permitted him to drift in the same way he'd done there forty years before at Trinity.

'You're down to hell,' Mido Cooligan used to say to him as he looked at the examination board. He'd laugh as he listened to him, just as he'd laugh when Uncle Whiskers was down to hell, or 'down the field,' as he put it. Maybe that was where all the best people were, and the best horses.

He's nearly fifty years dead now but I still think of that Friday when I sat in my seat in the Savoy cinema watching 'The Omen,' going into Eason's afterwards for the book he asked me to buy him on Hitler, then walking home with it in the rain, not knowing what was waiting for me.

People sometimes ask me to define him in a phrase. I tell them I'd need a million of them, because he was a man for all seasons. And, being Irish, they changed by the day.

I think of him these days every time I see James Cagney in a film, or Edward G. Robinson, or Ramon Novarro or Ivor Novello. I think of him when I see white scarves and pinstriped suits, when I see someone swinging an umbrella or wearing a monocle.

I think of him when I see a poorly produced court drama on television, with a 'surprise witness' being trotted out in the final reel to knock the prosecution's case for six. He's sitting watching it from his bed and then he jumps up and takes his pipe out of his mouth and shouts at the television, 'That wouldn't happen in real life!'

I like remembering him when he was at his happiest, rocking on the balls of his feet as he told some hoary old yarn, saying, 'Be gee it was good, wasn't it?' after it was finished as he forced you to agree that it was even if you didn't think so.

He was my role model not because he was perfect but because he wasn't. I knew I could never approximate to my mother's perfection so I sought solace in him instead, finding in him a mirror of my own contradictions.

After he died I went in search of other role models. Sometimes I found them and sometimes I didn't. When I didn't I tried to make sense of life on my own messy terms.

That's still going on today. I still don't have any answers. I've just stopped asking the questions. It's a different kind of reaction to life's problems, the acknowledgement that most of them can't be solved.

Whenever he was trying to figure out the finer points of something he used to say, 'Fools ask more questions than wise men can answer.' He was right about that.

I'm thankful I had him in my life through all the good times and the bad ones, the highs and the lows, the agonies and the ecstacies. He wasn't someone who tried to attempt answers to life's conundrums. He was more interested in questions than answers too, even if it made him seem 'foolish.' As he often said, quoting one of the many lines of poetry he seemed to have at his fingertips,

Shakespeare had one of his characters define life as 'a tale told by an idiot, full of sound and fury, signifying nothing.'

At times he felt that way too. At times we all do. If we're lucky we see flickers of light, flickers that might become constellations one day, the small glimpse of fire igniting a much bigger one.

Have I found anyone to replace him? No. But he lives on in what he's left me. He lives on in the way I think and feel, both about him and the life he lived, about the world he left behind him and the one he inherited, the death rattle of one and the birthpangs of the other warring inside him like the pincer grip of his own dichotomies.

Maybe W.B. Yeats put it best when he said,
'Now that my ladder's gone,
I must lie down
where all the ladders start
in the foul rag-and-bone shop
of the heart.'

www.ingramcontent.com/pod-product-compliance
Lightning Source LLC
LaVergne TN
LVHW020051110826
845155LV00021B/63

* 9 7 8 1 9 1 3 1 4 4 7 3 9 *